Alfred Hayes

The March of Man

And Other Poems. Second Edition

Alfred Hayes

The March of Man
And Other Poems. Second Edition

ISBN/EAN: 9783744709620

Printed in Europe, USA, Canada, Australia, Japan

Cover: Foto ©Thomas Meinert / pixelio.de

More available books at **www.hansebooks.com**

THE
MARCH OF MAN

AND OTHER POEMS

BY

ALFRED HAYES

AUTHOR OF 'THE LAST CRUSADE,' 'DAVID WESTREN,' ETC.

SECOND EDITION

London
MACMILLAN AND CO.
AND NEW YORK
1892

All rights reserved

CONTENTS

	PAGE
THE MARCH OF MAN—	
CANTO I	1
CANTO II	75
DIES NON	140
WELCOME TO THE QUEEN	147
SPRING SONG	155
A CHRISTMAS CAROL	156
MORNING TWILIGHT	159
THE SEMPSTRESS TO HER SKYLARK	160
SEMPER EADEM	162
THE DEAD CAPTAIN	166
WITH FLOWERS	167
A STORM SCENE	169

CONTENTS

	PAGE
To One in Sorrow	171
To Sweet Seventeen	172
Grass of Parnassus	174
Autumn Song	176
Serenade	177

THE MARCH OF MAN

Canto I

BLIND—then a little light—and once more blind.

Blind in birth's living shroud, there blindly reared,

Thence blindly driven—and lo! a drowsy babe,

Its red face wrinkled like a fresh-blown poppy,

Whose silken petals keep awhile the crease

Of every fold they slept in. Day by day

The light grows friendlier, till the strange great eyes,

So vastly vacant, so profoundly grave,

Stare hopeless, fearless, loveless at the world.

Then dawn of soul and day of strength, then dusk

Of fading dreams—a sigh—and once more blind.

From darkness unto darkness; and this hour
Of shattered lanterns and of naked lights
Doth but the more reveal the enfolding gloom.
What recked our brute forefathers of the cave?
They slew and ate, begat and slept; to them
Earth seemed not one stale cradle, one stale tomb,
Floating untended through the boundless void;
The weakling's moan, the spoil of lust and rage
To them brought no misgivings; and we saints,
We sinners, curbed and bridled into crime,
Our tender souls self-tortured with remorse,
Envy them oft their blameless guiltiness.

Death grins at birth, and birth makes mock of
    death;
Death, birth, and death—O weary, weary round,
If self were all!—to think it, is to droop,

To live it, is to die. Away with self!

Not beasts of prey, but human hearts of love!

Not claws of greed, but eager hands of help!

Not civil foes, but comrades in one cause!

Forward!—we cannot backward, if we would—

Forward through law to righteous lawlessness!

The generations pass into the dark;

They fold themselves in silence, and are gone;

Their loves and hates, ambitions, wrongs and tears,

Pangs of the body, puzzles of the brain,

Vex them no more. In vain our men of light

Dissect the living nerve, in vain our priests

Plead with the God of old, in vain our seers

Question the heart of mystery—the deep

Gives back no answer, and the ghosts that thronged

Faith's morning-twilight visit not her noon.

Noon? — rides the sun so high? — or lingers low

Beyond the horizon, while we wisely take

Marsh-lights for stars, and starlight for the prime?

Those altars yet outface the storm, whereby

The gaunt white-bearded prophet of our sires

Stood, drenched with human gore; he doubted not

His night was day; and we, who hail some few

Pale streaks of morning, howsoever fair

And fraught with promise, for the light of noon—

That open glory of the sunlit heavens,

That desert-dreamland moving as we move—

Are blind as he, and children of his pride.

Yet Progress doth not halt, but holds her way,

O'er dust of ancient wisdom, power and wealth

O'er palaces whence kingly pomp hath fled,

And temples where dishallowed gods lie low,

Heavenward. The soldier sinks, the host moves
    on;
It marches o'er the dying and the dead,
Tramples, but after worships; for the fallen,
Whose closing eyes through cloud of battle-smoke
And mist of death beheld the promised land,
Are foremost conquerors.

                    The march of man
Lies through a mountain-region; each life-path
Leads o'er a mountain's brow from vale to vale.
Some slumber in the vale of infancy;
Of such as climb, some choose the lower path
And some the loftier; some the storm-bolt slays,
Some stumble o'er the precipice, and some
Sink overtired and perish in the snow;
The loneliest victor of untrodden peaks

Descends at last into the vale of age,

Weary and travel-worn; and lays him down—

With boys that wonder at the next white peak,

Restless to climb—beside some placid pool,

And dreams it doth not move. But on the heights

Stands Manhood, firm, erect, alert, and tracks,

Ere he too fall asleep upon the shore,

The windings of the stream of Time, now seen,

Now hidden, backward to its secret source,

Forward to shining visions of the sea.

For Time is not a whirlpool, but a stream;

It hath its eddying cycles, cataracts,

And quiet-gliding deeps, with here and there

A backward current born of overhaste;

But the whole mass of waters onward bears

Toward, who shall say what dream of golden peace,

Or, if our sadder moods forbode the truth,

Toward silence, darkness and forgetfulness—

What then? The world is young, and who would shrink

To play the man, though death indeed close all?

We perish, but the victory lives on;

Our eyes grow dim, our hearts grow faint, the sword

Shakes in our grasp; we yield it to our sons,

Bless, send them forth, and lay us down to die.

Old age doth well to guide, restrain and warn,

But youth is the true prophet; the hot heart,

The eager eye, the ecstasy of faith,

The joy of daring—these have won the world;

And he that hath them, being old, is young.

Children of light, arise!—the shadows flee,

The daylight is at hand!

．   There was a noon
When Rome's imperial eagle, poised aloft,
O'erawed the savage West; then darkness fell,
And in that darkness greed and lust grew fat;
Children forgot to blush, women to weep;
Whole cities thronged to see men bleed for gold;
The rabble fawned, the noble tossed them bread;
The good and true chose death; a pool of gore
Reeked round the throne, and each bloat murderer
That sat thereon was God.

                            Into the midst
Of that foul gloom a lowly beam of light
Stole from the East, and steeped in sacred blood
Slowly prevailed and widened into day;
The breath of life swept through those fetid mists;
Christ's Vicar sat in Cæsar's seat, the slave

Leapt from his chains, the brothel-temples fell,

Cathedrals rose to Heaven like prayers in stone,

And kings paid court to holy men who wore

The Master's crown of thorns, ate of the field,

Drank of the brook, and preached in loving deed

Good tidings to the poor.

      Then once again
Fell darkness; prelates clutched the sword and
  purse
Black with the ban of Christ, hid reason's star
With smoke of reason's martyrs, turned the halls
Of brethren bound in equal helpfulness
To dens of harlots. They whose crippling toil
Made sleek the lord, robbed of their wretched
  bread,
To swell his pomp, ate grass and lay like swine;

For him the court, the dance, the chase, the feast,

The rape of maiden brides; for them the load

Of hopeless days, the halter and the wheel.

Dense was the night, and angry was the dawn;

Fierce smote the day-star reason on the pride

Of Pope and King;—it melted like the rime,

And thought took wing once more.

                        Then glared a noon

Of terror, and the death-light of eclipse;

And in that lurid gloom a nation strove

Single against the world, and all the Earth

Was shaken with the thunder of the strife.

The would-be Cæsar fell, and night returned

Haunted with echoes of old ruins fallen

And fitful levin of the people's wrath.

The promise of that dawn, "No more of chains!

Brothers and equals all!" was born in blood;

Blood ruled the day, and blood defiles the night;

For in this lingering night, while louder swells

The shout of revel and the roar of toil,

While wail and threat of misery disturb

The rich man's peace, and idle palaces

Forbode the earthquake, while the nations groan

Under their weight of armour—fools and knaves!

We trample happiness, to clutch at gold

Wrung from the slow starvation of the poor,

Profess the Christ, and plead the plea of Cain,

"Each brother for himself."

                                Night lingers yet;

But darker hours have passed, and even now

Faintly, but widely, glimmers the new dawn.

We shall not see its glory, we who strive

Sad-hearted in the spectral twilight, sick

With long soul-hunger, weary to behold

Greed seize his shivering prey, and in his web

Mammon the subtle spider lurk, his paunch

Swoll'n with the blood of bright and wingéd things.

We shall not see the glittering halls of guile

Totter, the homes of honest toil grow fair,

The couch of selfish sloth become a bed

Of loathing, and the labourer rise and shake

The vampire off that sucks his weary veins;

We shall not breathe the loftier purer air

Of civic life, each emulous for all,

And all for each, when none need strain or starve

That some may surfeit, none be vilely clad

That some may blaze with jewels, none be choked

With highway dust that some may lightly toy

In flowery glades of sweet unfruitfulness;

When cities shall no more screen dens of slaves

With bowers of indolence ; but stately halls

Of Art and Truth shall rise 'mid beauteous homes

Of brethren banded for the common good,

Faithful in toil and just in recompense,

Simple of life and strenuous of soul,

Through union strong and free through self-
restraint,

A wiser, nobler, lovelier race than ours.

It dawns, but ah ! how slowly ! and what clouds

Of sloth and hate, of dullness, pride and greed,

Obscure it from our sight !—Yet see ! the hills

Are crowned with splendour, and the wistful eyes

Of them that watch thereon are full of fire

Children of light, arise !—the shadows flee,

The daylight is at hand!—fulfil your dreams;

Up to the hills and view the growing dawn!

Your dreams have given it birth; see that it live;

For ye are guardians of the day, its glow

Springs from your hearts, defenders of the faith,

Bright champions of the noble, just and true!

Cry to the poor, "Ye shall not always pine

In darkness, cold and hunger, while life's feast

O'erflows for them who make their heaven your
 hell!"

Cry to the drudge, "Thou shalt not always rest

The thing of scorn thy lord hath held thee, slow,

Long-suffering, hard and stubborn as an ass,

Stunted in soul and brutal in desire,

Ill-fed, ill-housed, coarse-featured and coarse-
 tongued."

Cry to their lords, "Ye have betrayed your trust,

Put to base use your basely-gotten gains,

Have lured the blind astray, enslaved the weak,

And given their bread to rascals; ye were called

To lead the world in loftier ways of life,

And ye have served your bellies and become

A byword and a blot; your days are told."

Cry to the bountiful, "Your wheat was sown

'Mid tares; one sickle reapeth all; fear not;

The harvest will divide the tares and wheat;

Blame not the reaper's hand; so suffered Christ."

Cry to the stubborn, "Tremble for your sons!

On them you lay the burden of your debt;

They shall redeem it; flatter not your pride;

Redress is sure; only with you it lies

Whether it come of reason or of wrath."

Cry to your loitering brothers, "Up! and join

Our slender band, one day to be a host!"

Take sword and shield; the powers of night are
    strong,
The battle will be long and bitter; sound
The clarion of your faith, "Christ lives, no more
In shrines of stone, but in the hearts of men!"
The wiser poor, the kindlier rich, will hear
Your summons gladly; and the wavering throng,
Catching amid a thousand doubtful cries
One clear firm trumpet-call, at last will seek
Your standard, and the victory will be yours.

Sound an alarm! for many a waking soul
Listens, while comfortable captains drone :—
"Loud fools, that think to fashion gods of clay,
Let be! ye vex yourselves in vain : the dawn
Asks not your aid; ye cannot stay its course
Nor hasten it one hour."—Regard them not;

Prophets of ease, ambassadors of sloth,
Seducers of the soldiery of Heaven!
They spake not thus, whose voices echo yet
Across oblivion's widening domain,
Those mighty marshals of the wars of old.
Man's spacious evolutions on this world's
Dim battlefield, where night contends with day,
Spare not a soldier; each one doth his part
To make or mar the triumph, and he thwarts
Who helps not. None can watch the shifting lines,
The headlong rout, the struggling hero-band,
The heights now gained, now lost, 'mid curse and prayer,
Wail of the wounded, silence of the slain,
Himself unmoved, save Him who moveth all.
Love's kingdom is not won by watching; Heaven

Is slowly scaled by toil and tears and blood;

The bonds that man hath woven man must rend,

The wrongs that man hath suffered man must right,

The hopes that man hath wrecked man must restore,

Man's nobler order man himself must found.

What though in bygone æons some vast power,

We darkly name by the great name of God,

Scattered the seed of systems through the void,

Spake to them, "Thus and thus ye shall unfold,"

And left them self-sufficient but foredoomed

To one fixed course?—the destinies of man

Revolve not as the planets round the sun,

Move not to music of some distant sphere,

But answer man's own impulse, and are ruled

By human passion, pity, faith and love.

The goal we cannot choose but reach, is seen

By human hope and sought by human strength;

The laws we cannot choose but own, are writ

In human hearts, proclaimed by human wills;

Fate's active servants, not her passive slaves.

What though, engendered in Time's secret womb,

The germ of all that man shall ever be

Was quickened by the Maker and ordained

To see the light with labour and with groans?—

Yet knowledge can assuage the pangs, and skill

Hasten the joyful birth. What though the world

Untimely suffer many a spasm which fails

And brings forth nought but sorrow?—every throe

Hath yet its purpose, and unknown prepares

The agony which yields the newborn life.

The old world lieth quiet in its grave;

Castle and abbey crumble, gently falls

Decay's gray breath upon them, and the ivy

Stealeth a silent triumph o'er their death ;

The new world striveth blindly to be born ;

The dungeon-bars are sundered, but the dens

Where hirelings sweat dishonour frame and soul ;

The chains of steel are snapt, but weaker slaves

Groan under stronger lords in chains of gold ;

The lance hath rusted, but the arm of wealth

Wields mightier weapons, hunger, cold and shame ;

The Wonder-god departeth, but the faith

That drave him forth hath fled the minster-walls

And wanders outcast, homeless and forlorn ;

So, when his pity of the bruised and poor,

His wrath against the proud, had won for Christ

A felon's doom, the warders of his truth

Spake not in temples rich with carven stone,

With incense dim, and hallowed by the prayers

Of ages, but proclaimed from meagre rooms

The gospel that availed to cleanse the world;

It hath its temples now; the faith to come

Shall dwell therein when wider day prevails,

A thousand dawn-hues blending in one light;

And who shall say, when that bright dawn is seen

As darkness, what transcendent noon of faith,

Pure, open, boundless as the blue of heaven

The future shall disclose?

                                 The nations writhe

In travail, and a smothered moan is heard

That shall become a mighty cry and shake

Men's hearts with joy and horror of the birth.

Slow is the labour, for the birth is great;

Bitter the pangs and sick with baffled hope.

A hundred years have pondered on the throes

Of her whose haste proved hindrance, when the torch

That Luther held to heaven, and Cromwell snatched

To kindle a great people's zeal, inflamed

A stormier neighbour, and the right of self,

Unchained at last, amazed to feel its strength,

Turned freedom into frenzy, and so wrought

New shackles of the old.   A score of years

Unpondering have trampled on the sod

Where sleep the soldier-craftsmen of the Seine,

Untimely bold, whose battle-cry was yet

The watchword of the future—"All for All."

Slow is the travail, and no child of ours

Shall greet the newborn day; he shall but see

The bosom of the nations heaving hard,

Perchance some fierce convulsion that shall make

All Christendom turn pale and gasp for breath,

While year by year the rich shall grow more soft,

The poor more stern, the strife for gain more wild,

More hopeless; wealth shall league with wealth, and want

Shall league with want, till that strange hour ascend,

When one shall hold within a trembling palm

The substance of ten thousand marshalled slaves,

Each wiser, trustier, manlier than himself.

Slow is the travail, but the birth is sure;

Resistless forces muster; myriads aid

The great deliverance, neither knowing it

Nor willing; the rash strife of selfish aims

Hath served to bind men closer, and beneath

The tribulation of this pregnant age

Is felt the throbbing of a nobler heart.

The birth is sure.

     The pilgrimage of man

Is toward his godhead; long the way and steep;

And gazing on the heights that tower before

He well may droop, but gazing on the plain

Where once he trod, take heart. The World to
  Come,

The Fellowship of Toil, the League of Right,

The Reign of Love, the Commonwealth of Peace,

Could scarce seem stranger to our eyes, than we

To the wild naked race from whom we sprang.

Man that shall be half-god was once half-beast;

He ate his kind, he pierced the withered womb

That bare him, flayed his foe and grinned to mark

His dying torment. How might such as he
Forebode an age to come, when man should spin
Rock into less than gossamer, weigh the stars,
Bridle the lightning, wield the thunderbolt,
And bind a girdle round the loins of Earth;
While Art should lift and Faith should fire the
    soul,
And gentle hands should wait upon the sick,
And all the tender charities of home
Hallow man's life? Brutish and slow and few
His purblind promptings; yet a root so base
Hath borne at last such blossom; and shall we
Who wear it, and who know the savage soil
That nursed it, wring our hands because its thorns
Are strong and cruel, crying, "Alas! in vain
The warmer sun, the kindlier air; in vain
We vex our richer clay; the seed we sow

Will spring no quicklier than the seed of old,

Will yield no fairer flowers than these we pluck

With disenchanted hearts and bleeding hands?"

None may peruse the book of things to be;

But we, before whose eyes the fading Past

Lies like an open scroll, may well divine,

Reading the breathing records of our day,

Some phrases of the page our sons shall write,

Cancelled, confused, o'erwrit, its fairest words

Blotted and blurred perchance with tears and blood,

Yet bright with hope, and everywhere inscribed

The watchword of the future, "All for All."

Man hath misused the powers a god might boast,

Hath turned the ties of helpfulness to chains,

And lord of wind and wave and fruitful field

Is slave of greed, till now, ten thousand years

Of conflict overpast, his millions dwell

Less sweetly than the bird that year by year

Sings as he builds amid the budding thorn.

Ages of bitter penance must redeem

His long transgressions and instruct him late

To use his gifts aright; blood yet may flow

In freedom's cause, as ofttimes blood hath flowed,

But blood will ne'er cement with lasting strength

The stronghold of our peace; it will not stand,

Till conscience-struck the rich at last renounce

Their deathful privilege of sloth and waste,

The poor awake from stupor, and the light

Of conscious power and hope illume their souls.

Then shall its broad foundations rest on faith,

Love shall combine its parts, and justice rear

Its pillars, and all hands shall gladly join
To stablish and adorn the home of all.

Brothers in toil and triumph ye shall be,
Bright children of the future! nevermore
Hungry to plough that gluttony may reap,
Naked to weave that vanity may wear,
Homeless to build that idleness may lounge;
No more to wallow in the mire that some
May dally in the meadows; nevermore
To stint the heart and starve the brain, that some,
Your ceaseless sweat sustains, may mock your
  prayers,
Sneering, "The swine would have us cast them
  pearls
To trample."—Courage, friends!—beneath the
  froth

Of light and glittering wavelets, backward tossed

By fashion's puffs, one all-embracing tide,

Mighty as truth and deep as righteousness,

Holds, inch by inch, its unrelenting way.

Lo! how its sway advanceth! Wave on wave,

Steady and buoyant with unfathomed depth,

Hath rolled across the leagues of heaving grey,

Hath risen and reeled and fallen, and seething
    dashed

The rattling shingle up the shore, sucked back

Only to speed the further.
                     Many a year

That flood hath rolled since when the German sage,

His grave eyes warm with pity of the poor,

Watched the yet ebbing tide, and them that left

Their cabins 'neath the cliffs to pitch, with slow

And bitter toil, beneath the lash of want,

Pavilions on the sand, where Ease might sport

Softly secure.   He watched and groaned and spake ;—

" Weak thralls that toil, strong lords that rob and waste,

It will not be for long ; the tide will turn,

And slowly flowing swallow with its surge

Palace and hut alike that rest on sand ;

And naught shall last which human hands have reared,

Till Justice build her temple on the rock."

So spake the seer ; men stopped their ears and scoffed ;

But in these latter hours, while deep the dust

Lies in his grave, along the wide world's marge,

Distant and low, is heard the approaching roar

Of overwhelming waves, till myriads now
Unstop their ears, and harkening, some with fear
And some with hope, confess the prophet's truth.

Swiftly for many an age portentous powers
Have leapt from darkness, urging unaware
The tide of toil's redemption; for the wretch
Who wandered naked, couched him with the wolf,
And slew his sons to glut the fiend of storm,
Now speeds through mountains, cleaves the hurricane,
And speaks across the ocean; while his soul
Mounts ever higher;—no longer brutes that snatch
Their solitary prey, but kindred wills
Combining widely for a common good;
No longer slaves, branded and bowed and blind,
Of lords that live by plunder of the poor,

But freemen marshalled close and firm, to claim
Through majesty of labour's calm revolt
Salvation for their fellows, space to breathe,
Light to rejoice in, time to muse and feel,
And not by never-slackened strain to prove
Unwilling thieves of one another's bread ;
Salvation for their masters, wholesome due
Of daily toil, sound brain and honest heart,
And not with jockey, drink and drab to spill
The sacred gold which is the blood of men.

Over the troubled waters of the world
Broodeth a newborn spirit, that shall calm
Their self-destructive conflict and call forth
Order again from chaos. Far and wide
Resounds the cry,—" Enough of self's mad fight,
Enough of blaring each his brazen lie,

Of hewing at our brethren in the dark,

Of trampling on our allies in the rush;

Let us be friends, and working with one will

Possess the earth whereon we now but bleed!"

So rings the cry;—and what though many a soul,

Untouched by passion for the public weal,

Swell it through guile or fearfulness or greed,

Nursing some narrow end? What though the crowd,

Unmindful of the cause that is mankind's,

Bleat but as sheep that hear their flock-mates bleat?—

"'Twas ever thus; the good cause basely served

Is good no less; the oak-tree thriveth not

By shower and sun alone, but by the blasts

That shake its heart, and by the rotten mould
Of its own leaves that falling feed its strength.

The temple of the future hath its base
Deep in the past; the master-builder, Time,
Slow to upraise from naked wandering wights
The tribe that owned one sire, from tribes the town,
From towns the nation, and from these the race,
Will found at last the Fellowship of Man.
Shame on all hearts that feel, all souls that think,
And hold this rich estate of life in trust,
If careless of the increase yet to be,
Forgetful of the increase that hath been,
They idly eat of others' toil and so
Renounce their stewardship! Shame on all eyes
That read the record of man's uphill march
Heavenward, from when he ate his kinsman's flesh

Till when his spirit soared in flights of song,

Surveyed the pathways of the stars and curbed

The lightning for his courier—shame, if we,

Who enter on such lordly heritage

Of act and hope, fold idle arms and whine,

"The world stands still ; the wrongs our brethren
 bear

Are cureless as old age; the crushing loads

We bind upon the shoulders of the weak,

The helpless girls on whom we wreak our lust,

The little ones that starve to swell our feasts,

Loud hawking of false wares, perpetual toll

To him who toileth not from him who toils,

The mill-horse round from dusk to dusk, till
 heart

Shrinks, and the soul stagnates, and the brain
 throbs

To the engine's pulse, and man becomes machine,

The itch of greed, the haggard overstrain,

The senseless rivalry of costly show,

Stupor of ignorance and sloth and want,

Fever of gaming, harlotry and drink—

These things are everlasting; man hath learnt

By sore experience much; but never hope,

Fond dreamer, men will learn to cast the slough

Of selfishness, or steadfastly to lead

Righteous and watchful lives, or toil to enrich

The common treasure-house and win for each

His portion at the banquet spread for all."

Shame on the faithless ones who thus disown

The promise of the past! The goal indeed

Is distant; many an age must bleed and sob

In greed's unthrifty fray, ere wisdom's light,

So faint and fitful yet, illume the world,

And men be schooled to help where now they hate.

The goal is distant, and the straining limbs

Of them whose eyes descry the promised land

Will never rest within it ;—but the hope,

The striving, dies not with their dust ; they send

Their sons afield, lithe limbs and eyes of fire,

Sound brains and hearts of sunshine, and they cry,

" God speed the young ! they start from where we sink ;

Bravely they run the race wherein we faint ;

Their breasts are heaving with our hopes, their feet

Fledged with our conquests ; and when age hath warped

Their thews and chilled their veins, and when their eyes

Swim, straining at the future, from behind

They'll hear the rush of feet, and as they fall
Gasp with their latest breath, 'God speed the
    young!'"

Yet ponder, ye who dream the reign of love,
The coming Christ and Kingdom of his peace,
Are nigh; Justice must first prepare the way,
Or Love will trip; and Justice tarries long.
Dulled with the long day's fight for meat and
    drink,
The crowd are but as babes, that heed alone
The wrong that pincheth their own flesh, the
    fear
That knocketh at their own barred gate by night;
Let lust and greed and malice wreak their worst,
Let war and waste devour the garnered grain,
Oppression stalk unchallenged, fraud grow fat,

Perish the sun, moon, stars, yea! perish God,

If but their cushioned cradle rock secure.

Such are the crowd; howbeit the human bond

Was ne'er so strong and ample, nor the lie

Of Cain's lean creed so blank. From land to land

Speeds lightning-winged each nation's joy and woe,

A million brains quick with the selfsame thought,

A million hearts hot with the selfsame hope,

One mind, one soul, one purpose, and one law.

The wide world trembles in her strength, aware

Of some great doom impending; the old cry

Of "King or People" faileth, the new cry

Riseth of "Rich or Poor"; the slaves that tax

Sinew and brain to feast an idle few,

Bound in one league of patient self-control,

Strong with the meat of wisdom slowly won,

Bold with the wine of righteous discontent,

Will one day hold of Mammon's stewardship

A searching audit; slowly will redeem

The monstrous debt which centuries of wrong

Have heaped upon the poor, or with one stroke

Cancel it evermore; will wisely change

By just degrees the fashion of the scheme

Of human toil and recompense, or stung

By misery and maddened by disdain

Shatter it with a blow—The rich may choose.

No more the father of the church constrains

The pride of wealth, the rage of lust; no more

The priest, once champion of the people, curbs

The gilded tyrant; and no power stands forth

To play the umpire in the fierce free fight

For gain, and summon with controlling word

The struggling throngs to order; and no faith

Of all men held inspires, no hope of Heaven

Gladdens the heart of misery. The faith

That fired all France, and glowed through half the
    world,

A hundred years gone by, was strong to shake

Old fabrics, but it founded not the new;

Madly it flung the rusty forms of life,

Sceptre and crest and crosier, into scorn's

Fierce melting-pot, but the fresh shapes are yet

Uncast, and slowly must the metal cool

In firmer moulds of thought, ere once again

Order and faith prevail. Liege-lord and serf

Have yielded place in gain's ungoverned strife

To millionaire and hireling, every man

A law unto himself; these too shall yield,

By slow advance of firmly-planted steps,

To common labour for the common weal,

Rich store and right award of honest wares,

To common learning for the common good,

To faith and hope and care of humankind,

To larger aims and broader ways of life,

Till "Each for Self" shall yield to "All for All."

A hundred years gone by, from shore to shore

The Western deep resounded with the clang

Of sundered chains; Britannia's eldest-born,

The sturdy babe delivered from her loins

In pangs of persecution and despair,

Grown to a giant, cast indignantly

The leading-strings aside that vexed its strength,

And shouted "Freedom!"—France caught up the cry,

And gave it tenfold breath, proclaimed for naught

The chance of birth, the pride of place, and drew

With fiery hand, and held to all the world,

The charter of her faith, the Rights of Man.

Kings trembled, nobles quaked, and priests turned
    pale ;

The powers of darkness gathered ; host on host

The thunder-clouds of battle rolled their gloom

Toward that strange light, and like the levin's flash

The sword of France leapt forth. Then gyves,
    that long

Had galled and rusted, fell ; prelate and lord

Fled naked ; thought and deed, till then held in

By rotten reins, burst them and rioted

Stark mad ; and ere that lurid sun went down

In reek of luxury, the wakened world

Had welcomed a new gospel, "Off with chains !

Free fight on a fair field, and devil take

The vanquished!"—Good! so that the field be fair,
So that the combatants be justly matched;
Good!—and we bless the day that gave the West
A spur so sharp; good!—but a better waits.
What comfort to the millions who must sell
Their toil for aught the hour affords, or starve,
The chapman standing by with tongue in cheek
Watching the teeming strife which works him
    wealth—
What comfort that we dub the bargain free?
Free as the brigand choice, "Your gold or life,"
Free as the hounding of a naked horde
By armed battalions. Little need to-day,
Whate'er our grandsires' need, to preach the faith
Of selfish claims; the nobler faith be ours
Of civic duty, and the steadfast hope
Of that good time when none shall gloat o'er gain

Wrung from the helpless, but each man's desire

Shall be the public weal, and all shall dwell

In healthfulness of mutual toil and rest.

Yet thank we gallant France, who singly bore

The onset of the tyrants, leagued to quench

The torch she held aloft to light the earth.

Forgotten be her sins—mitre and crown

Provoked them, and the red-cap's rapid axe

Dealt gentler torture than the noble's wheel—

Remembered only be her rich bequest

Of reason to the nations; let all time

Record beside the ruins she o'erthrew

The monuments she reared, and how she waged

Fierce but triumphant war with all that checked

The flight of thought, and how her prophets heard

Beyond the castle's doom, beyond the din

Of Mammon's palace rising from its wrecks,
The footfall of the serried ranks of toil,
The murmur of the Commonwealth of Peace.

"Away with lord and slave! be comrades all,
Brothers and peers and freemen of one realm,
Knit in one faith, advancing in one hope,
Ruled by one law of labour, light and love!"
So rang her clarion-call, startling the world.
What though too soon the wrath of rival powers,
The crash of cities and the war-bolt's scream
Drowned that clear voice; what though the nations yet,
Unmindful of the cause that is mankind's,
Arm horribly in silence, and 'neath brows
Burdened with care and darkened with distrust
Glare upon one another?—the new Word,

Announced in storm, inscribed in tears and blood,

Will be fulfilled in peace; the dead leaf falls,

The young bud gathers strength to burst its sheath,

Not in wild nights alone, but genial hours

Of showery sun and days of frosty calm.

Firmly the people's master-hand doth mould

The stubborn clay of custom to new shapes

Befitting the new needs; slowly the sway

Of force and fortune yieldeth to the sway

Of thought and toil; and surely the grim fight

For daily bread of those who would be friends,

That rageth round the holds where age by age

Mammon hath piled the plunder of the poor,

Worketh the slave's salvation; stealthily

Greed, trembling for the safety of his hoards,

Heaps them in fewer strongholds; foes within

Contrive their rivals' fall, and foes without,

The hungry hosts that surge around the walls,

Compass them ever closer; and more loud

Than yell of hate, or groan of agony,

Riseth the cry of hope,—" Comrades, be strong,

Patient and bold and true; the better time

Draws near, when they alone shall reap who till

And sow and tend the harvests of the world,

Not they who lounge and waste!"

So rings the cry,

The one heart-utterance heard in every land,

The one clear message from the world to come;

It soars above the rage of factious strife,

The wrangling of the market and the courts,

The wail of dying creeds and wandering calls

Of marsh-light mystics, and will lead mankind,

Obedient to his own unfolding law,

Through many a slough, o'er many a stumbling-block,

To righteous ways and plenteousness of peace.

Closer and ever closer all that is

Binds man to man; he cannot, if he would,

Renounce his brother's charge, or tread alone

The path of his own choosing; the old faith

Departeth; the free fight of "Each for Self"

Hath lost its fierce confusion, and in haste

Rangeth itself in two vast leagues, of them

That have, and them that have not; nor shall these

Make common cause till o'er one mighty host

Shall float one stainless ensign, "All for All."

Far off! and yet 'twill be! if not more soon,

Yet not less surely than this anxious age

Hath blossomed from the wildness of a past

As base as we shall seem to eyes unborn.

'Twill be ; the age of single aims will pass ;

The world-soul waketh ; gambling-hell and stews,

The worldling's palace and the wage-slave's den,

Will fall and fade like evil dreams away ;

'Twas not to reach a Heaven so low, that saints

Have wrestled, poets sung and patriots bled ;

They toiled and suffered for a somewhat higher

Than self, for that great Being which doth enfold

The ages and endures beyond their death,

In Whom we live and learn and ever move

Onward, Whose sight is faith, Whose breath is
    hope,

Whose dwelling is eternity, Whose power

Is blended of all passions, thoughts and acts

That spring from noble natures and achieve

By slow degrees salvation for mankind.

Our path is 'neath the storm-cloud; but though mists
Perplex and darkness daunt us, yet beyond
The battling winds, the blindness of the bolt,
The sobbing rack, is seen a glimpse of blue—
The promise of a holier day than ours,
The portals of the City of Content.

Two thousand years have billowed o'er the day,
Nor worn its deep inscription from Time's shore,
When on a Grecian plain the powers of Night
Were scattered and the shackles of the East
Sundered for evermore; Freedom that day
Received her charter, and the People's cause
Blood-baptism, and the young West learned to soar
Where yet she had but crawled, and sought and won

The cloud-crowned heights, and made the chariot-
    wheels
Of progress glow, till now at last she draws
The laggard Orient in her train, and holds
Upgathered in her hand, some dangling loose,
Some tightly stretched, the reins of the whole world.

The dead of night is past, but the new dawn
Not yet hath roused the sluggard; Tyranny
Hath doffed his robes for slumber, and no more
Shall do them on; the rich young fool, made drunk
With vanity and vice, securely dreams
The wealth he never toiled an hour to win
Is his for ever; swindler, niggard, churl
Heavily breathe; but hark! what boding sound,
A sound of limbs that stretch and breasts that sigh,

Is heard the wide world o'er!—at last—oh! hour

Long waited for by them that watched and strove—

At last their ears have heard the trumpet-call,

At last the light hath pierced those weary lids,

At last the workers waken!—Tempt them not,

Ye, whom their nakedness hath softly clothed,

Ye, whom their slow starvation hath fed sleek;

Sleep on, and let the hungry millions tramp

Unchallenged past your tents; or, if ye wake,

Out of their path, as o'er the Gallic bounds

Your fathers fled; and see ye stand not by

With listless smile or academic sneer

To mock their rude requital; they have told

Your lavish lusts and strictly reckoned up

Your debt of folly; let them not require

Of you the silver hairs their sires ne'er saw,

Of you the bread their little ones have lacked,

Of you the blood their simple sons have shed,

Of you the honour from their daughters torn;

Yield them thus late their own, the fields they till,

The wealth their toil hath fashioned; and thereto

Add fervent thanks if haply they should spare

To claim arrears, if haply in some hour

Of generous triumph they should reach the hand

Of fellowship to all men—even you.

But if with stubborn dullness ye should baulk

Their progress, and the billows of their might

Thwarted in vain should rise and overleap

All natural bounds, devouring in blind haste

Evil and good alike, forgetting him

That wisely put his wealth to noble use

And left his ease and joy to serve the poor,

Remembering only the fat drones that filch

The gathered honey of the human hive

And scorn the work-bees—can ye blame their wrath

That pauseth not to winnow? Hath your caste

So singled out, when time and chance were theirs,

From the rough ranks of toil the man whose soul

Was as a lamp, dusty and soiled, yet lit

From the great Sun, or hath it stolen the light

And trampled on the lantern?—dare ye say?—

Howbeit when those seventimes beleagured walls

Fell to the trumpet-summons seventimes blown

Of Israel's captain, she whose casement showed

The scarlet thread, one friend amid the foe,

Was rescued, when the conquering hosts poured in,

For one good service, she and all her house.

Therefore be wise in time, and have a care

By large endeavour for the public good

To turn the blade of vengeance, and make smooth

The path of peaceful conquest for the hosts

That thunder at your city gates; take heed

To shed abroad the truth ye cannot quench,

Lest light turn lightning; flatter not your souls;

Ye hear afar the murmur of the flood;

There yet is time; but if ye stop your ears,

And cry, as cried the loathsome king, whose breath

Poisoned the air of France, " Let the cup's chink,

Loud folly, and the laughter of bought love,

Drown yon low menace; give us leave to sleep

And sin away the remnant of our days

On beds of ease; then let the deluge come!"—

If thus ye hug your comfort, your sons' blood

Be on your heads, haply your own blood too!

Haply the rotten dykes will not outlast

Your own poor shred of life; the suffering throngs

Grow shrewd, and will not evermore endure

To clench the idle hands that fain would toil,

To meet the mother's piteous eyes, and watch

The silent children gaunt with stint and cold

Huddle their rags around them, while the lord

Who boasts the land his own whereon they pine,

The gamester of the mart who wrings close rent

For dens where rats would sicken, the wage-monger,

Whose ground of vantage is the wage-slave's need,

Wastes on his cook the gold that would have fed

A score of craftsmen, while his brainless heir

Squanders among the rascals of the ring

A city's revenue.

                The men who pay

With brain and thew forced tribute unto such,

The men who feed and clothe and deck the world,

The jaded hacks of labour, busy-blind,

Will pause some day, and stand with folded arms,
Waiting amid the silence of the wheels
Till right be done; nor will they wait in vain;
The people's cause is just, and late or soon
Will triumph; slowly dawns, through slavehood's
　　night,
The quickening truth that all who sweat for hire,
With thew or brain, are brothers in one bond,
Seared with one brand, bowed down beneath one
　　yoke,
Wistful with one dumb hope which stammers now
Toward utterance, troubled with one blind desire
For better things. Their cravings shall not rest
For ever unappeased; closer each day
Toil's dense battalions muster, and their foes,
Foreboding the long fight of rich and poor,
Would sound a parley, learning wisdom late.

The issue who can doubt?—If thought and toil
Make strong, if vice and indolence make weak,
If justice, truth and honour be not dreams,
The wrong will cease, the nobler day will dawn.

A day of world-wide peace and rich content,
Of rightly portioned toil and due repose,
Of honest comradeship whose "mine" and "thine"
Waiteth on "ours," of knowledge freely shed,
And wide communion of awakened souls,
Of simple manners flowering from one field
Where common work makes common wealth—that
    day
Will surely dawn and cast athwart the world
Shadows to us unknown; new sun, new shade.

And oft the spirit questions if man's life

Holdeth more joy to-day than when he ranged
A hunter o'er the wastes that knew no lord,
And flushed with chase and breeze and sunshine caught
The wild maid by the hair, and made her his
In lawless solitudes, and thought no wrong.
Soul-sickness was not then, nor doubt's lone chill;
The strain of living dulled not life's keen edge;
Loss tore no heart; death was a wayside thing
Scarce heeded; and the savage, if he lacked
Our costly heritage of art and thought,
Yet knew not what it is to hear the clod
Knell on the coffin where some brain that burned
With youthful ecstasy lies cold, and feel
The world within one sob, the world without
One hungry void.

Therefore what profits it
To banish grosser forms of want and woe,
If finer spirits suffer finer pains,
If crime but yield to subtler shades of sin,
And evil's sum abideth? What avails
The conflict, toil, and patience, if the end
Be only loftier heaven and deeper hell,
Not that good time we seek?

The promised land
Is ever on the verge; yet, laugh or weep,
We cannot choose but seek it; and the speed
Makes our hearts bound and fills our lungs with
    life;
And as we journey on, sunshine and cloud
Will smile and frown more evenly, and men
Breathing one air, illumined with one light,

Will hold each other dearer ; and the best

Of joys, the joy that knoweth not remorse,

The fellowship of kindred souls, will spread

O'er the glad earth like common flowers of Sprin

Such fellowship we know not ; for what help,

What common hope or joy, can knit the heart

Of him whose life is one stern fight for bread

To him whose only care is how to tempt

His jaded appetites, can win the love

Of her who nightly sews herself a shroud

For her whose gravest thought is how to deck

Her dainty charms anew ?—The selfsame wrong

That starves the poor man's soul sickens the rich

With surfeit, and dismays the heart of them

Whose modest portion seems now lavish waste,

Now penury.

I

The goal whereto we press,

The far-off fellowship of quickened souls,

Is past our ken; nor will the eyes of man

Behold it till the fruits of all men's toil

Are shared aright; till none are bowed like beasts

By ceaseless strain, but truth and art have blest

Each cradle; till the holds of selfish pride

Are levelled, and the wise and good alone

Are held in worship; till by dint of pain

Mankind hath learned 'tis better and more sweet

To serve than rob and wrangle, and the temple

Reared by all hands is nobler than a batch

Of paltry huts. But till that bright day dawn,

Alas! how long!

And oft in darker hours

Weary we ask, "What profits all our care?

So dull and slow the crowd; so deep the chasm

Dividing churl from gentle; the gross beast—

Slave of the prize-ring, gambling-hell and stews—

From Thought's throned kings; the hag who lays
    her snare

For maidens' feet, from the pure ministrant

By dying beds; so loudly roars the mob

Of sluggards, fools and cheats; so dimly shines

The lamp of truth and virtue through the gloom;

So slowly through the generations' veins

Pulses the nobler blood; so light the leaven,

So huge the lump—a soul that thinks and feels

Were best outside the turmoil; life is sweet

In the calm shelter of a cultured home;

The friendly hearth, the love of wife and child

Close commune with the teachers of all time,

Deep drinking at the deathless founts of song

The care of flowers and fruit, the master-strains

Of harmony, the stately walks of art,

The wonderland of science—these suffice;

And sweet to wander through this English land,

By mead and orchard, copse and old-world grange

Lulled by the song of brook and bird and bee;

And sweet to watch the pale green moon of May

Rise o'er the tender larch-wood, silvering slow,

While dies the throstle's song, and the faint scent

Of young leaves after showers fills all the soul

With longing for some delicate romance,

That like the horizon's dreamland evermore

Eludes embrace."—Ah! we could dwell at ease

In life's fair upper chambers, could rejoice

In life's continual music, conscience-free,

But that the same fine sense, which apprehends

Each subtlest note in her rich symphonies,

Hears, saddening all, a dreary undertone,

The sigh of them that surfeit wearily,

The wail of them that daily build and tend

The palace of our joy, but when we feast

Lie cowering in its dungeons; we could keep

Delicious revel with the shapes that haunt

Soul-slumber, but that ever and anon

Some ghastly scene of want or waste or greed,

Some wretch that slays her infant for the gold

Wherewith to drug her misery, some villain,

Falser than fox and earthlier than hog,

Who cheats the poor to roll in costly filth,

Bursts through the lovely texture of our dream

And wakes each honest passion; and we call

On all who hold by justice, truth and love,

To quit for one short breathing-space the roar

That drowns the single voice, join hands, and take

This simple oath, and teach it to their sons,

"Never through grief or joy to flinch or flag

Till right prevail, till all men justly share

The sweet and plenteous fruit of all men's toil,

Till knowledge, art and gladness be as free

As sunlight, and the gulf 'twixt lord and slave,

The coarse and fine of manners, garb and speech,

Sunder our lives no more "—this oath to take,

Then back into the tumult and the wrong,

And mend it in God's name!

'Tis not enough

To till our little plot, to greet our friends,

To purge our flesh and feed our soul—to play,

How graciously soever, with the life

That is the curse of thousands. None can live

Unto himself and sin not; help he must,

Or hinder, man's salvation; and what spirit

So mean as his who, when his brother groans,

Mutters, "I harm thee not; my dream is good,"

And turns again to drowse?

                                      Awake, awake!

Ye that have brains to ponder, hearts to feel,

And hands to help!—awake, and let your dreams

Melt as the morning mists; gird on your swords

And forward! linger not; your time is short,

The march is long and toilsome; greater need

That ye, who are the vanguard of the host,

Should strike your tents betimes; and never doubt

That Man will some day reach the land he seeks,

Nor deem, because your path is dark and steep,

Beset with foes and pitfalls, the great name,

Unknown of old, whereby the ages move

In steadfast order, marshalled by one law—
The mighty name of Progress—a vain sound.

Not all man's pride, unwisdom, sloth and sin
Can stay mankind's advance; the tyrant's scourge
Doth but unsheathe the patriot's sword; and
    Greed
Grasps at his own destruction. The old days
Are gone, when solitary nations grew,
Flourished and fell like desert palms; when she,
Even she who taught the West to build and rule,
And well-nigh knit the ancient world in one,
Could shake it with her downfall, and no sound
Startle that undiscovered world to come,
Where but the red-skin roamed. Man made not
    then
The hemispheres his pleasure-ground, nor raced

The blasts from shore to shore, nor flashed each
    hour
The lightning message of his weal or woe
A thousand leagues through voiceless depths of sea;
The poet's word, the thinker's scheme, the strain,
Past speech, past thought, of Music's mighty sons,
Thrilled not through all the nations till they grew
The heirloom of mankind; but every realm,
The lordliest and the wisest of old days,
Lived to itself alone, and so decayed.

The doom is changed; Science and Art and Trade,
Yea, War herself, have woven round the world
A web so strong and subtle, that the lands
Are veined and nerved to one great heart and brain,
Are limbs of one World-being, and the wrong
That grieveth each becomes the wrong of all.

No more we lead the narrow single life;

The globe is now our storehouse; day by day

We steep the leaf and berry of the East,

We reap the golden harvest of the West,

We greet our kin who dwell three thousand leagues

Beneath us. Broadly Progress plants her feet,

Stumble she may, but naught can hold her steps,

Till that far land, the glory of whose light ·

Glows in her eyes, be reached, where none shall eat

Who labour not, where just award of toil

Shall win for all repose and joy, where greed

Shall bow the neck to help, and strife at last

Shall turn to peace, and wrong to righteousness.

And murmur not if they, who hold this faith,

Seem to the crowd, that deem the age they see

The pattern of all ages yet to come,

Dreamers;—so be it;—the temple of mankind

Is reared by them that toil and fight and die

For noble dreams, not them that yawn and sneer.

Hated, derided, trampled by the feet

Of hurrying throngs, spurned by the hoof of fools,

Tortured and starved and slain, but at the last,

When all he loved is unto him no more,

Believed and reverenced—the dreamer knows

And seeks his doom, but sees beyond all clouds

The eternal sun, and feels within his soul

The secret pulse of everlasting life.

Forward !—what matters self, if but one spark,

Quenchless throughout the ages, help to kindle

The beacon-fire of truth, or light those souls,

Still brooding o'er the ashes of the past,

With flame from a new Heaven? What matters scorn,

Sorrow or death, if but our brothers learn

To quit the couch of pride and sloth and shame

And draw the sword of right, our sisters learn

To kiss no more the wounds of a dead Christ

But speed his second coming?—One by one

The weak waves leap and dash their troubled breasts

To pieces with a moan upon the rocks—

And yet the ocean conquers.

Courage, friends!

We stand as on a summer night when long

The sun has set, and mark the deathly pallor

Still lingering o'er his grave, and half forget

That there the newborn day will rise—but see!

The dubious dusk, that wraps all thought and deed,

Wherein we grope and stumble and lament,

Is yielding to a steadier light, and they

That watch upon the peaks have seen afar

The gleam of a new dawn; portentous clouds

Roll thither, and the powers of gloom would quench

The promise of its glory; hues of blood

Flush all its brow with wrath, but swiftly fade,

And tenderer tones prevailing shed their glow

Wide o'er the gladsome earth, and evermore

Increase in power and warmth and loveliness,

Till emerald, sapphire, ruby, gold and pearl

Are blent in one clear diamond of the day.

Canto II

Are we but babes, that, meeting Mother Truth

In strange attire, we bellow first our fear,

Next timidly draw near her, lastly crow

Ecstatic credence, till some newer garb

Fright us; or own we Nature's kindly care,

That lets the sere leaf shield the tender bud,

Till the young life hath gathered strength to thrust

The old life aside?—When he, who late descried

The slowly sure unfolding of all germs

Of being, proclaimed the now unchallenged law,

Fools scoffed, priests shrieked, and good men
shook their heads;

"A blind black mole, that burrows in the soil,
And sees not his snout's length, would sap forsooth
The very citadel of God."—So now,
When heralds of the wondrous change to come
O'er toil's wide world announce the gradual dawn
Of justice and the slow redress of wrong,
The piercing of thick darkness by thought's lamp,
The melting of old icefields by love's sun,
The ceaseless long ascent from savage greed
To full community of lofty aims,—
No more the wild-beast impulse, "Clutch who can,"
But in the mart and street the self-same law
That blesseth home, the rule of "All for All"—
When thus our seers foretell, the jostling crowd,
Blind with the dust, deaf with the din of toil,
Revile them, "Fools and rogues! that think to shake
Wealth's firm foundations, build of common clay

A pleasure-house for all, and people it
With angels!"

Thus the crowd.—But they who know
That every bud will blossom in its hour
Can wait for springtime calmly. The base strife
That rageth in the market-place is seen
To winnow grain from chaff, the man of might
From weaklings; and the chaff, fools take for grain,
The loud-lunged trumpeter of lying wares,
The cunning spoiler of toil's simple slaves,
The idler who grows sleek while labour starves,
A mightier fan—the people's righteous wrath—
Will some day scatter.

But a nobler strife,
That ceaseth not when other battles fail,

Prepares a holier conquest ;—bruised and worn,
But vanquished never, wresting evermore
Their fencéd places from the powers of gloom
That slay themselves, the soldiers of the light
Hold undismayed their course. Hope fires their eyes,
Faith nerves their heart, and love makes strong their arm ;
Their very foes applaud them, after death
Hath sheathed their sword, and rally round the flag
Once mocked and trampled ; and each age shall see
The muster-roll of dull and sordid souls
Dwindle, of lofty souls and wise and true
Swell evermore, till selfish cunning yield
To social truth, and darkness unto day.

Growth governs all things; and the headlong rush,

The conflict and the eddyings of life's stream,

Are but as sap that frames and feeds new forms

Still to unfold; not virtue's self abides

Constant; to let their vengeance fall asleep—

Christ's law—his fierce forefathers held a sin;

To rend the nerves and roast the limbs of them

That caught and clasped a purer truth, seemed once

God's bidding; and an hour will surely rise

When the gross blots that yet defile man's life

Will fade; when they whose fathers thought no shame

To gloat o'er others' ills, and harboured dwarfs

To mock at, will as soon deny their guest

His portion at their feast and snatch at all

That hand can reach, as round the board of life

Shoulder their neighbours from the common store

Like hogs around a trough ; will rather choose

To trample down a cripple in a throng,

Than make the helpless hunger of the poor

A vantage-ground to rob them ; rather dare

To slay by force a feebler than themselves,

As in old days, and batten on the spoil,

Than squander in vain show the garnered fruits

Of others' care, and watch their brethren strain

Joyless and hopeless through the unvarying days,

That they may riot. Such growth will come to
    light ;
And coin which passeth current in our streets

Will then be deemed base metal.

                               That calm seer,

Who widest hath unfolded the great scroll

Of human doom, foretelleth a far day

When Nature, careful evermore to guard,

Through mother, lover, patriot, martyr, saint,

The unselfish type, will yield from these at last

Love's triumph and the Polity of Peace.

Fitness alone surviveth; ay! but who

Shall gauge the fitness,—God or Devil?—Fit

To tear at one another's throats? Or fit

To wisely rule this world of tooth and claw,

Which yet is man's high empire, wherein claws

Have sheaths, and teeth have lips to smile and kiss,

And help o'ermasters hate?—To sway such world

Not they are fit who grasp and waste, but they

Whom Greed itself, while mocking with its mouth,

Worships at heart,—the generous, just and true,

The scorners of all base pursuit of gain,

The lovers of all things that lift the soul,

The loyal to their city and their land;

These shall abide, the others pass away;

These—for the world around him, moulding man,

Is by man moulded—shall possess the earth,

Shall fashion it, from age to age, anew,

Begetting still of goodlier heritage

Yet goodlier heirs; shall slowly wean Mankind

From Strife's dry, bitter breasts, to feed and smile

Upon the bounteous bosom of sweet Peace.

Nor only through dominion of high souls

Is toil's release accomplished; Avarice

Weaves unaware his winding-sheet; in vain

The profit-monger wringeth the last drop

From the pinched toiler's heart, in vain would rend

His victim, like a beast of prey, unwatched;

His hungrier rivals scent the spoil, and some

With roar and leap, some crawling like a cat,

Snatch at it piecemeal, and when all is gulped

Prowl o'er the blood-stained spot, their green eyes slant

With envy and mistrust, unsatisfied;

Till now they take late counsel, and henceforth

Would hunt in packs but eat in solitude

The portioned quarry. It will not be; their prey

Have learnt like cunning, and from far and near

Compass with ordered hosts the scattering gangs

Of seekers after spoil, and will not blench

Till all the field be theirs.

       'Tis done—What then?

When the long strife is over, when the gulf

'Twixt rich and poor is filled, when each pursues,

Obedient to self-love, his brother's good,

And " All for All " is sovereign—what remains
To hope and toil for?—Fear not; heights beyond
Our short horizon then will tower afar,
Tempting to effort; scarcely hath man spelt
Through nature's alphabet, whose magic book
Holds in each word a universe; scarce kissed
The hem of art's rich robe, and scarce explored
A single creek of music's welling stream,
That whispers now along the reeds, now laughs
O'er pebbly beds, now roars below the rocks,
And lastly flows, a broad majestic flood,
Bearing the souls of millions with its tide,
Into the main of song.—'Tis much, that now,
Even in these murky days of greed and want,
Beauty hath smiled and wisdom turned her lamp
On thousands, where till late all things were dark.
'Tis somewhat—and the commune of such souls

Is life's best boon ;—but when the promised sun

Hath risen, and equal laws and manners shed

Their genial influence o'er the minds of men,

Growths sweet and strange shall flourish, blossom-
 ings

Undreamt-of deck the highways hateful now

With tumult, dust and blood ; and human souls

Shall know an intercourse more wide and free,

More lofty, true and delicate, than aught

Our dullness can imagine ; genius then

Shall burst its chains ; no longer shall bare want

Turn men to beasts, the sordid strife for gain

Shrivel and starve the soul, nor idle riches

Gorge it to slumber ; Fortune's foolish sons

Shall lift no more a languid brow of scorn,

Nor lackeys do them worship ; but each man

Shall move amidst his peers, and frankly meet

His neighbour's gaze, and find him, not as now
In guise and bearing, thought, desire and speech
An alien, but a fellow. Fancy then
Shall browse at large, wisdom enrich her store
Ten thousandfold ; art, like the gladsome sun
Revealing, through the gray, heaven's boundless
    blue
And earth's fair shapes and tints, shall mount her
    throne,
Scatter night's sullen clouds, and light the world ;
And music, like the common flood of life,
Well in the hearts of all men.

                          But till then,
Alas! how long ! What mountains to remove
Of wretchedness and pride ! Through what dense
    thickets

Of tangled ignorance to hew a way!

What barren wastes of sloth, what rocky wilds

Of crime and madness, what death-reeking swamps

Of lust, what sloughs of sottish selfishness

To traverse, ere the land of hope be won!—

Little it serves that he, who, dawn to dark,

Is bondslave to the lords of soil and steam,

Chinketh more pence, to flatter his dull brain

With tavern fumes, than his poor sire could count,

Dying a young-old man in sterner days

When war made bread a dainty; little it serves

If, while the drudge starves seldomer, his lord

Heapeth from others' patient servitude

A pile of gain, that viewed in hungrier times

Had seemed a kingdom's ransom;—the deep chasm

Yawns ever deeper; the rich man knoweth not

The bitterness that gnaws the poor man's heart,
Nor he the other's loathing, but each dwells
In thought and speech, desire and deed, apart;
Where faith should be, distrust; where mutual help,
An ever-widening conflict; little serves
A fuller belly for the slaves of toil,
A vaster luxury for the lords of wage,
If that for which alone all gold is gain—
The free and equal fellowship of souls—
Be not a whit the nearer.

      Light is good—
And blesséd be the bravely wise, whose names
Are beacons for all time, who suffered scorn,
Torture and death, rather than quench the spark
That burned within them—light is good—and well

That science scanneth all things, that those dens

Where reverend goblins lurked are merry now

With children's laughter—but not light alone

Can guide the erring steps of man aright,

Or heal the hurts of ages. Fain would France,

In that fierce glare which flashed along the world

A hundred years gone by, have spread her wings,

And clutching all the West with eagle claws

Have soared to Heaven on one broad beam of
  light.

Alas! the wings were glorious, but the claws

Were claws of prey; and that whereon they seized

Was solid flesh and dragged her down to earth.

Not darkness only hinders; Truth's worst foes

Bask in full sunshine—Indolence, that lies

With nerveless limbs and half-closed lids, and gapes

At the blue main above him, where the clouds

Set their white sails and chase their snowy sisters,

Majestically slow; Pride, with firm foot

That pauseth where his shallow eyes may greet

His image in the stagnant pool; old Custom,

That grazeth without pause in sheltered croft

Where grass is deep, and with a paunch well filled

Settles his heavy bones, and hour by hour

Cheweth the cud untroubled; Jealousy,

Lean-cheeked, slant-eyed, whose hunger grows more fierce

By feeding; Lust, with trembling hand, that clutches

The crystal cup wherein the wine of life

Sparkles, and breaks the cup, and wastes the wine;

Greed, whose small eyes survey his bloated form

And rest content—such are the foes of Truth.

And Truth's defenders, who for her pure sake
Renounce their ease, forget their pride, forego
Tradition's downhill slope, abandon fame,
Bridle each lust, and serve not their own good,
But single-hearted live and die for Truth—
How few! and through what struggles, wounds and tears,
What pitfalls scarce escaped, what lonely hours
Of failure and mistrust, they keep their faith.

The same clear light, that beaming from their souls
Shines on the land of hope and leads them on,
Reveals the unheeded snares and stumbling-blocks
That baulk the feet of Progress, bids them teach
Their eager hearts the unregarded law,
That only by one all-accordant will

A host can march in order, and each foot

That trips delayeth all ; too well they know,

The nobler order will not come to pass,

Nor, founded, will endure, till age on age

Of pain's strict schooling soundly hath informed

The minds and hearts of all men ; till strife cease,

Till every frame be strong and beautiful

And every soul be true ; and since but few

Of many paths, that part along the road

Where darkling man doth grope his dubious way,

Lead to the realm of righteousness—nor these

The smoothest—many a wrongful age must pass,

Ere from the loins of them who wander now

From virtue's way, and lured by marsh-lights sink

In sin's contagious slough, is born a race

That walks aright as surely as the flower

Turns to the loving sun.

How long to wait
Till that full day, the wisely-good best know;
And they who hold their lives in constant pledge
To speed its rising, need not faith alone,
But strength to plough the trodden ground of Use,
Courage to sow the seed 'mid storm and gloom,
Patience to wait its growth, and at the last
Contentment to reap little. Well may he
Endure with joy the martyr's pains, who cheered
And blinded by hope's dazzling beams expects
A quick and plenteous harvest; but foreseeing
The glory of a future which his eyes
Shall ne'er behold, and knowing with what slow
And ceaseless pains the tillage yieldeth fruit,
How distant the due season, and how weak
The mightiest striving of a single age
To foster good—this knowing, yet to ply

With warm and steadfast will his thankless task—

This marks the hero; and the faith of such

Assures its own fulfilment
.

       Forward! then,

With courage, but with patience, sons of light!

Firmly but slowly let your footfall sound;

And while your brows are lifted to the heavens,

See that your steps be sure, your course be straight,

And while your standard presseth to the van,

Remember still the rear, and hold your ranks.

Ye shall not reach the promised land alone,

But one and all; the world's old footsores first

Must heal, the foul be pure, the false be true,

The churl be kind, the drunkard reel no more,

The brute be tamed, the bigot raise his lids,

The dreamer wake, before those city gates

Open, where neither lord nor slave abides,
But freemen only.

              Not the subtlest scheme
Contrived by all the wisest of this world
Can shape the course of things; the good will
    grow
Its own dark way; we can but watch and tend
Its slow increase, and tending heedlessly
May check it, and uprooting some rank weed
May tear the fibres searching through the soil
Where evil feeds with good. Howbeit, to tend
The slow and secret growth of good aright
Craves no unworthy husbandman; the clay
Is heavy, and the field is thick with tares;
Shod must he be with patience, robed with truth,
Discreet of purpose, diligent of hand,

And in his heart—as in the heart of that
Strong singer who foretold 'mid Israel's woes
The kingdom of her peace—must ever glow
The vision of the labourer's recompense,
The golden glory of the harvest-home.

There was an age, whose records rudely graven
Are wellnigh worn away, when bulk and thews
Alone were sovereign, and the large of limb
Trod down the slight, as some huge river-horse
Tramples the reeds beside an Afric lake—
An age of dwarfs and giants. Slowly forth
From that gross gloom a gleam of cunning broke—
The weakling's weapon—and from more to more
Grew, till the strong were fain to learn its use.
Lastly, than force and cunning mightier far,
The power of fancy rose; in weight of limb

II

The desert brute o'ermasters man, in skill
The spider may perplex him, or the bee,
The pinion of the soul is man's alone;
And urged on fancy's wing, reason hath sought,
Espied and won new empires, till man's spirit
Mounts like an eagle, every beat of wing
Revealing vaster prospects, and yet soars,
Amazed at the wide wonder of the world.

Time hath unclasped his volume to our gaze;
Spellbound we scan those pages which the Past
Hath hallowed with its finger, and we see
A mellower glory flush them than the light
Which glares upon our page; but when the hopes,
The strivings and the triumphs that we know,
Are gray, no page will seem to after men

More fraught with majesty and high romance
Than that which beareth witness of our day.

Lords of the waves, compellers of the winds,
The common usage of our life outstrips
The wizard's wildest dream; Nature herself
Hath done us homage, and the deeps of space
Disclose to us their secrets; we have made
The thunderbolt our minister, and hold
The powers of flame in leash; our fiery steeds
Ascend the mountain-side, and on those heights,
Where clogged with snow earth's proudest soldier
 crept,
Rush snorting through the rock.

       With awestruck eyes
The simple Eastern mariners of old,

Coasting along their tideless sea, beheld
Long billows from an undiscovered world
Roll slowly in, and, where the god of strength
Had fixed his pillars, leap against the rocks,
Bound thundering back, and waste themselves in
    foam.
The baffled East withdrew, but lent the West
Her balanced needle trembling toward the pole,
Pilot, o'er pathless wastes of wave and wind,
To that vast ocean-mainland where a man
Might hold his faith untroubled by the frown
Of pope or king.

                 Through many a changeful age
The white-winged messengers of war and peace
Traversed that mighty solitude, till now
Our prows of steel each hour 'gainst storm and tide

Cleave their appointed way, and the twin wires

Flash at a kiss the tidings of our weal

'Neath twice three hundred leagues of restless brine;

They lie—those sister threads that link in one

The Old World and the New World—where no light

Nor sound nor motion liveth, mantled o'er

With finest snow of shells, so delicate,

A breath would crush their fabric; overhead

The blasts do battle, and the writhing clouds

Weep with the waves. The levin's rage is tamed

To light our midnight musings and give back

Forgotten accents of the mouldered dead;

The sun is made our limner, and the stars

Reveal their unseen splendours unto eyes

By man contrived, that see where man is blind.

We watch the shapeless embryos of systems

Fashion themselves in the vast womb of space,

We see the gnat's heart beat, and 'neath our lens

The water-drop becomes a peopled realm.

The loom whereon the weaver slowly wrought

His simple web has grown a living thing;

We give the word, and lo! the shuttle flies

Unerring, while deft fingers of bright steel

Catch at the threads and weave a damask sheen

Subtler than winter's handiwork.   The blind

Receive their sight; the days of man increase;

The knife hath lost its terrors, and performs

Its office calmly, while the sufferer lies

In merciful oblivion; the dark laws

Of birth and death are searched.

        Thought, free as light,

Enters at last the hovel; they who drudge,

From dawn to dusk, forgather in the dark,

Look in each other's eyes and find a soul,

That long time flickering soon will burst in flame;

A silence holds the hosts of toil, like that

Strange silence, broken here and there with sobs,

Which fell upon the negro in the night

That saw his slavehood ended; dumb he knelt,

Trembling to take possession of his life,

Till midnight's last stroke, and the sudden day

Of heaven's white fire-flash, and the salvo-peal

Of thunder echoing through the fateful night,

Proclaimed him slave no more. Even such a spell

Holds labour's troubled legions; but they wait

A like deliverance, and fulfilled at last

With one strong pulse of common grief and hope

Beckon to one another o'er the seas;

Hunger and cold and darkness have not quenched

Their spirit quite. With all its wrongs and woes,

This age of iron is the age of thought,

This age of labour is the age of love.

'Tis somewhat that our stature hath outgrown

The mail our fathers wore, that week by week

A thousand bloodless battles on the sward

Tighten the thews and purge the blood of youth

And drill the civic spirit; and glad of cheer

We mark the lamp of learning more and more

Make the dark places light and waken souls;

But chiefly we give thanks that man hath caught,

Even in the midst of greed's inglorious fray,

Clear glimpses of a nobler life, and sees

The hunger after righteousness and truth

Plead in his brother's eyes, and grasps his hand,

And cries, "Thy cause is mine."

Our laws are cast
In larger moulds, no longer shaped to please
A tyrant's humour or a prelate's pride,
But fashioned by the people's sovereign will ;
And that which, voicing forth men's dumb desires
And formless thought, is mother of all laws—
The poet's word—no longer adulates
From taverns, loud with cackling wits, the rich,
But communes in sincerity of soul
With nature's heart and man's ; no longer struts
In wig and lace, sham of a sham, but breathes,
In music broad and free as ocean's roll,
The mighty yearnings of this wonder-age.

Firmly the people's wider grasp doth seize
The heaped-up measure of the nation's wealth
And shake it slowly level ; toil and rest

And health and joy shall be in days to come

Common to all as sunshine; stumbling-blocks,

That evil men or dull have set or left

To trip their brethren's feet, the wise and good

Still gathering strength will one day overcome;

And natural ills, birth-stains of frame and soul,

Nature herself—who mother-like chastiseth

The child that spurns her laws, but mother-like,

If he repent, kisseth the smart away—

Will surely cure, if but we thwart her not.

We shall not hear the triumph-song resound

In that sweet city of peace, nor our sons' sons

Shall view its stately splendours—for the world

Is younger far than old—but blind is he

Who deemeth not this age of vast design,

Of snapping chains and soaring thought, the prince

Of all the ages past; and base is he
Who takes no joy, forecasting how the page
That tells our tale will some day thrill the souls
Of happier men redeemed through our distress.

Therefore we lose not heart, but ever press
Forward, remembering that the lordliest tree
Was once a seed and thrust through stubborn soil
A pair of pallid leaflets toward the light;
Remembering how each unfamiliar good,
Which braveth frost and tempest now, will grow
Old in its turn, and when its wholesome strength
Is wasted and decayed, how they will most
Uphold its age whose fathers hindered most
The promise of its youth; knowing that heights
We vainly strive to scale will yet become
Highways. And though the slow advance of things,

Like some broad-moving flood, seemeth at times

To lose all patience, and with rush and roar

Take at a leap the precipice and ride

Triumphing over shoal and rock and bank,

We rather trudge than hasten, wotting well

That only after many an angry bar,

And many a tedious bend, the stream of time

Will smoothly widen to the wished-for sea.

Too well, alas! we know the goodliest husk

Of civic rule is bootless, if the core

Of private life be foul; yet tainted rind

Makes rotten fruit.   We seek no single cure

For Earth's ten thousand evils; yet disease

Heals not itself unhelped.   We know, the road

That leads to Heaven is dusty, steep and long;

More need to start betimes.   Sadly we own

That Freedom's feet are blood-stained, and her eyes

Ablaze with frenzy; yet her soul is pure.

And like the sage who penned, when the red storm

Of France was at its fiercest, that calm page

Of mankind's heavenward march, we cheerly say,

"The sky is overcast, the thunder-god

Musters his sullen squadrons; but these melt;

The blue abides."

      The order we foretell

Is no raw scheme conceived in solitude

'Twixt woe and envy, but a gradual growth,

Sown by experience, planted in the past,

As labour wide, as hunger sure, and strong

As help itself; no system of the schools,

But a world-force. We boast not to discern

Each aspect of the changes it shall bring
O'er man's wide workfield—toil through law set
  free,
Greed's tumult ended, beauty's face unveiled ;—
Nor were they proven liars, who first proclaimed
The reign of steam, because they laid not down
The limits of its kingdom, imaged not
The rushing of our iron steeds by night,
Their white manes flaming while the riven rocks
And sleeping towns crash past them, and heard not
The hammer's mighty thud, that yet can crack
The wren's egg and not crush it, our sea-giants
Plunging through storm and darkness undismayed,
Or watched the ceaseless whirring of the wheels
Yield wealth ten thousandfold.—So we who preach
The mighty power of union take no shame
To own the prospect of the world to come

Hidden from keenest vision, but with clouds
Of glory.

We foretell a newborn age,
Begotten in the shadows of the Past,
Long nurtured in the secret womb of Time,
The hour of whose deliverance draweth nigh
In pangs and groans, perchance in wrath and
    blood;
Yet birth is but the promise of a life,
Not life itself; and that which sudden throes
Have brought to light, slow years of patient care
Must perfect.

The quick beat of Freedom's wings
Is heard as clearly by the ears that dread
As by the ears that hail it; and the sceptre,

Wrenched from oppression's clutch, the people's
   hand
Shall grasp with clearer wisdom, calmer will,
Shall ever wield more widely, till at last
Earth's fruitful workfields and fair pleasure-grounds,
Where age by age the poor have slowly shed,
To cloy a few, their bitter sweat and blood,
Shall be their own dominion.

                            Glebe and gold,
The pastures and storehouses of mankind,
Won in past ages, when the single arm
Sufficed, by lords who proved themselves in
   might
Best of their race, feed oft the sloth and pride
Of weaklings, fools and lechers, while the poor,
How wise or true or strong soe'er, are caught

In a tight snare of tangled circumstance,

Where struggling only maimeth.

But the curse
Shall not endure; the workers wake, and learn
That single strands, a child might snap, can twine
To cables; they shall weave a stronger bond
Than aught their lords have woven, they shall wind
Its coils about the tyrant, and possess
At last the world their care and thought and skill
Have fashioned and preserved.   Then Greed's
  fierce fight,
Rough schooling of a race half-savage yet,
Shall cease, its purpose served, and Justice late
Ascend her throne; labour and rest and joy
Shall be the blessèd lot of all, and none
Shall stint but rogues and idlers;—equals all,

Not in the gifts of nature, but the claims
Of brotherhood.

    Then not the chance of birth,
Nor hoarded gold wrung from the weak and poor,
But only the true kinghood of high souls,
The hero's glory, and the godlike brow
Of genius, shall have worship; then shall gladness
Course through the people's veins, as when the
  hearts
Of some vast throng are thrilling to one strain
Of lofty music; pleasure shall not need
To hide her eyes, ashamed that others' grief
Pays for her pastime; luxury's sick craving,
That owns no bound and therefore owns no peace,
That feeding but provoketh, shall be turned
To wholesome hunger, and lust's lawlessness

To wise and sweet restraint; and Earth's best
   boon,
The fellowship of hand and head and heart,
The commune of true souls, shall lighten toil
And heal life's deep divisions.

                              But such boon
Will never bless mankind till the dark gulf
'Twixt rich and poor, 'twixt sage and fool, 'twixt
   churl
And gentle is bridged over—for true friends
Are ever equals;—and that golden field,
That gladsome harvest of man's fellowship,
Now springing round our feet, will only reach
Its fulness after sunlight of free thought
And sunwarmth of wide sympathy have nursed
Its growth for ages.

Mankind's slow advance
From this misgoverned waste, where one man's weal
Worketh another's sorrow, to that realm
Where all conspire for all, is steeper far,
More toilsome, devious, and beset with snares,
Than aught his feet have traversed. They that lag,
Lamenting the old days, and they that haste
To greet the future, first must suffer much,
Much yield and much forbear, ere the long march
Be ended, and the promised land descried.

A weary way;—but whether with good cheer,
Or downcast eyes, we needs must take the road;
Backward we cannot; the world-powers that wait
Our nod, inwrought from land to land, no blow,

That spares this orb, can cancel;—the fierce giant
That leaps to life when fire and water wed,
Thunder's fleet daughter, and the subtle spirits
That mingle in Earth's veins to save or slay,
And mightier than all these, the living force
That beckons and controls them, the arch-force
Of human thought, of human love and will—
These are the people's weapons; armed with these
Toil's dense array shall hold its onward course,
Shall compass the strong places where the lords
Of wealth sit throned, and greed's inglorious sway
Shall fail, as failed the sway of cowl and crest
When learning woke, and art shook off her chains,
And commerce spread her wings, and thought caught fire,
And Europe had new birth.

The people's lips
Have touched the rim of wisdom's cup, and soon
Shall drink it deeply, till the sacred wine
Bound in their veins and fill them with the strength
Of giants; and the watchword "All for All,"
Uttered by millions marshalled in one cause,
Shall win redress for labour's heaped-up wrongs,
None daring to gainsay. But if the rich,
Drowsy with comfort, stop their ears, that watch-
   word
Shall heighten to a battle-cry, and wake
A conflict which shall grant no truce till toil
From the fat purse of idle luxury
Hath wrung the utmost farthing.

                        Pity then
For such as fain would put their needless wealth

To faithful use—the wise, the kind, the just;

Vainly they struggle, tangled in a web

That is not of their weaving. Oft, when ease,

High manners, and the pride of stately homes,

The healthful glow of roaming o'er the world's

Wide pleasure-ground, and all the finer joys

That blossom in the summer atmosphere

Of opulence, delight the rich man's soul—

The drear abodes of penury, where swarm

Gain's dull and haggard slave-hordes, suddenly

Loom round him; and he feels as one that quits

A feast, and, homeward journeying, while the wind

Fans his flushed cheek, sees shivering 'neath the
    hedge

An outcast woman gnawing a stale crust

For very life, the babe upon her heart

Plucking at empty breasts;—an alien she

In garb and feature, thought, desire and deed,

And yet a sister;—gladly would he yield

Some costly superfluity, to still

Her misery's reproach, but that his gift

Would seem a sand-grain cast into a gulf

That bounty cannot fill—" What use," he cries,

" To fling among the ravenous herd the store

Of my fair jewels?—Christ bade it; but the poor,

He spake of, were a handful;—had he known

Our coarse and grimy millions, stale with toil

And sour with sweat, that spice their drink with
    oaths,

Wallow in filth, and breed like sewer-rats,

He had not counselled thus.   Moreover, Christ

Lived upon alms;—the poor have ever preached

This gospel of renouncement to the rich;

And still the rich grow stronger, and the poor

Weaker; so be it; the poor, in life's hot fray,

Have yielded ground, they or their sires; while we

Enjoy the conquests of our fathers' might,

Conserve the nobler type, and, safe embowered

In park and palace, nurture stately bearing,

Calm thought and gracious speech, which else would die.

'Tis well; we do but yield assent to laws

That Nature made, not we."—So comforted,

And heaving a short sigh of half content,

Half pity, he fares homeward.

                                              But the poor

Have pondered it, and will not any more

Be cozened with this creed of Anti-Christ.

Man is not wolf or beaver, that the son

Should build as built the sire, each generation

Wrangle and filch as we; Nature disdains
A realm so narrow; and man's noblest powers—
Wisdom and might to tame the brute within,
Experience to live down his crimes and follies,
Skill to contrive what fancy hath conceived,
Harmonious effort toward a common good,
Reflection, foresight, sympathy, with all
That lifts him ever higher from the dust—
Are Nature's gifts, and unto man as proper
As cunning to the fox. Man's slow ascent
From bestial ways to dignity of life,
From war to peace, from wrong to righteousness,
From slavery to freedom, is no less
Nature's behest than that which bids the grub
Forget the crawling life of old, and wake
To find herself a winged and lustrous thing,
Companion of the sunbeams and the flowers.

Even so with man;—Nature hath not ordained

For few the butterfly's bright play, for most

The worm's ignoble wanderings, but wings

At last for all.

The sumptuous bowers, where Pride

Wasteth the slender substance of the poor,

Shall fall as fell Rome's drear magnificence,

And comely homes shall flourish where to-day

Are loathsome dens. The poor will learn to baulk

The rich man of his laughter when a score

Of desperate slaves contend to clutch the wage

Of one; will rather choose to rear a pair

Of sturdy saplings, spreading healthful arms

To breeze and shower and sunshine, than a thicket

Of stunted underwood. The man of toil,

Slow as a dray-horse, gentle, patient, strong,

Will cease at last to bear the monstrous load

Of others' pride, and wage for others' waste

The sordid strife we suffer, wherein he

Prevails, who bawling his false wares can lie

The loudest; will no more endure to see

His sons grow wan with hunger, toil and care,

His daughters seize the harlot's poisoned cup

For mere oblivion of the fetid den

Where Fashion's languid tyranny condemns

Her needle-slaves to pine.

                        The Greek of old,

Nobly impatient of the slave's harsh lot,

Sang of a good time coming, when the shuttle

Should labour of itself, and man be free,

His light toil o'er, to gladden his long ease

With dance and feast and praise of the good gods.

So sang the Greek;—and now the shuttle flies

Unhandled, and the tameless elements

Obey man's bidding, but by man misused

Heap, for the few, possessions past the lust

Of avarice, pollute the brow of heaven,

And leave the burdened millions a grim choice

'Twixt slavehood and starvation. He is robed

In softness, housed in splendour, and fed sleek,

Body and soul, with dainties and delights,

Who never wrought by sweat of brow or brain

The value of a crust; while he who bears

From dawn to dark the burden of the world,

Raises its harvests, rears its lordly roofs,

Clothes it with grace, and makes it for his master

A dainty pleasure-house, must fight to win

The rich man's leavings, dwell in sordid gloom,

And seek forgetfulness in flattering fumes

Of poisoned drams; his wife is gaunt with toil,

And pale for lack of sleep; hunger and care,

And pangs of travail, 'mid the ceaseless strain

To feed and clothe her babes, have gnawed away

Her beauty, and stern furrows scarred her brow;

Her eye is cheerless in her withered cheek,

Wanting the balm of tears—she hath no pause

To weep in, only day by day she drags

Her weary footsteps nearer to the grave.

But that sweet gospel of the Greek of old

Shall have fulfilment; not for evermore

Shall they who dream and paint and pen fair things

Alone be man's consolers, nor those only

Physicians of the wounded soul who drown

Its agony in music; but he too

Who schemes some useful wonder shall behold

His gift no more make tyrants of the drones,

And of the work-bees slaves, but win for all

Leisure and health and gladness—meed enough

For highest toil, if further meed be asked

Than the great joy of genius in its use,

That prompts the lark to soar, the seer to search,

The giant to stretch forward to the goal,

The thinker to lose fortune, fame and ease

For truth's sake, and the singer, toiling still

The livelong day for bread, to yet uprise

With dawn, and watch at midnight, for the love

Of poesy.

   He slanders humankind

Who doubts if men will toil, save to avoid

The goad of hunger, or to win the prize

Of riches wrung from others' misery ;—

Thinker and artist, healer, patriot, saint

Cry shame on him. Ev'n now the craftsman joys

To ply his craft, the strong man to put forth

His strength, albeit another reaps the gain;

Will he stand idle therefore, when the sheaves

Belong no more to slothfulness, the gleanings

To toil, but all the harvest is his own?

Taketh a man no pride to lead the chase,

Not lag behind, albeit the quarry slain

Is not for him alone; or doth the soldier

Shrink from the cannon's mouth because his comrades

Will share with him the triumph?—The wide world

Proclaimeth honour mightier far than greed,

And help than strife; from sea to sea the nations,

Choked with war's dust and wearied with its din,

Shout it to one another; and those hordes

That battle daily for a wretched wage,

To pamper idlers, make it a muster-word

For the great day of reckoning.

                              Wrong sits crowned,

But not for ever ; knowledge daily paves

The path for justice ; and though yet afar,

She cometh.   Happy he, who, when these storms

Have rolled away, shall dwell beneath a sky

Bright with the sun of righteousness ; then wealth

Shall not breed want, nor toil be slave to waste,

But all shall succour all ; then this vexed knot

Of tugging selfishness, this vast disorder,

This cumbersome excess of costly show,

This haggard strain, shall cease, and rich content

Shall spread her pinions like a peaceful noon

O'er the blest earth, and man be glad and free

Alas! but oftentimes the heart turns sick

With sorrow, and the eye of faith grows dim,

Marking the blind contempt of those that have,

The rage of those that have not; watching life's

Broad flood roll by, its surface sparkling free—

The fickle sport of sunbeam, cloud, and wind—

Its depths drawn darkly onward, where disease,

Lust and oppression, madness, hate and crime

Mingle their turbid eddies; and doubt crieth,

"So foul a stream will never lose its taint,

Nor reach the expected ocean; but ere long

The dykes will sunder, and some hideous deluge

Ride over all; and when that waste of waters

Hath washed Earth clean once more, a younger race

Will suffer, flourish, sin and fall as we;—

And so for ever—till the sick old planet

Grow death-cold, and the sun with all his train
Shock into Hercules."

.

      Sad souls there be
Who bode such evil.—Courage!—man, that knows
His days are numbered, doth not therefore fling
His cares and hopes aside, and let the thief
Plunder his store unchallenged. Humankind
Is sound at heart; the wise and good increase;
And chiefly gain's stern fight hath lent to men
Their cruel masks, which gladly they will doff
When strife shall yield to concord. Never hand
Hath wrought a marble god of common clay;
And not the holiest laws inscribed in Heaven
Can bind mean hearts to justice; yet if they,
Whose nobler promptings age by age have lured
Their brethren ever further from the brute,

Had held their peace because the brute-life pleased
The general herd, man had been wandering still
A savage in the wilderness. He chargeth
Men's bosoms with the lightning-flash who summons
From narrow seeking after narrow ends
To righteousness and justice; and the roar
That bursts from the vast throng, ten thousand hearts
Heaving as one, when some great patriot pleads,
Is stronger than the earthquake; petty aims
And paltry hates are drowned in that broad voice,
And all, exalted o'er themselves, will blush
Even to think the baseness each would act
Single and uninspired.—The very bulk
Of ocean, where the wind hath room to range,
Purgeth it, while the standing pond grows foul.

Therefore 'tis well that closer, day by day,

The wide world o'er, the sons of toil forgather,

And dreamers of a loftier life than ours

Utter their burning visions, and just souls,

Impatient of disunion's wasteful fray,

Rally their scattered powers, and pledge their faith

To lead true lives, to taste no pleasure wrung

From others' grief, but share the common load

According to their strength. What matters it

That they, whose hands have planted here and there

Oases in the desert of man's strife,

Lived but to see the sand-blast strip their palms,

The sand-drift choke their fountain?—'tis by stumbling

We learn to walk aright; had no star-seer

Mistold on Eastern plains the doom of kings,

We had not known the moment when the moon

Would mask her brow with shadow, or some wild

And bright-haired truant through the fields of
    space

Visit our skies once more. What matters scorn ?—

The record of man's triumphs is the tale

Of dreams at first derided, next assailed,

Lastly fulfilled. Where'er a young growth springs,

Down-trodden by tradition's heavy hoof,

There waits—the sap forced back to feed the root—

A harvest for the future.

                                Even now

Such harvest waxeth. They who, sick to see

Strife's blind self-slaughter, point to that fair realm

Where Concord spreads her feast for all who will,

Long mocked-at, then maligned, are now believed.—

None saith, "The world stands still;" yet that which moves
Must move somewhither; and what means this sound
Of labour's mustering legions, or these hands
That reach across a thousand leagues of sea
To succour a fall'n comrade, if the end
Be only the old reckless race to win
Self's goal by others' stumbling, if the city
Become once more the nomad's lonely tent?—
Madmen would wiselier dream—but if man's path
Lead not to self's inhospitable slough,
A sunnier clime awaiteth him, where, toil
Made light by union, thought and faith at one,
Hate overcome by help, and art uncaged,
Each soul shall breathe the same pure air and light,
And differ but in graces.

                    Blind are they
To Nature's beckonings who fear lest men,
Fattened no more on others' want, but bending
Their shoulders to the general wheel of toil,
Should lose the soul's distinction. Know we not
That bushman features bushman, driven to seek
The same base living by the same base means,
As wolf resembleth wolf; that thought and art
Then flourished first when mutual help had
    found
A swifter and a safer road to ease
Than single greed?—What space for growth of soul
Hath he who strains the deathlong day, to wring
From Mammon's clutch his wage of crust and
    rags—
Less valued than a horse—for if he die,
What then? another fights to fill his place;

But horses have their price?—depraved and starved,
Warped, numbed and stunted, how shall such as he
Put forth those beauteous blossoms of the spirit,
That purge indeed the air, yet will not bloom
Where all is foul and sunless?

       Wise were he
Passing man's scope, whose wit could apprehend
Each glory of the landscape that lies hid
Beyond our day's horizon—strange delights,
Strange griefs, strange hopes;—but, clearly to
  discern
Some wide and various harvest of the soul,
That waits the tillage of a nobler race,
And will not spring while of the husbandmen
Some filch the seed, some trample on the blade,
And most are stupid with the mill-horse round

Of sordid cares, or maimed with misery—

This craves no prophet.

                    Surely from the heat

That trembles in the world's deep soul to-day

Will rise new growths and lovelier forms of life—

Not suddenly, as when the metal cools,

The mould is cracked, and lo ! the statue stands;

But slowly, like the growth of a great tree.

The husbandman may train the boughs, may graft

A nobler stock to feed upon its strength,

But change its kind he cannot; husbandry

Maketh the crab yield pippins, never grapes ;

And those old promptings of the heart of man,

The love of home and kin, the joy to reap

The fruit of his own labour, howsoe'er

Their nature may be bent to worthier ends,

Are rooted in the ages, and though lopped

A hundred times will spread their arms anew.

We seek not to molest them—toil is good

And toil's reward—we seek to find for all

A place in the world's workfield, where good will

May win good recompense; we seek to stay

The spoiler's hand, and bid the idler yield

The sheaves he gathered not, that they may eat

Who labour, and the generous heart no more

Be bled by churls.

     Self-help is good ; but they

Who mark the trophies of man's care for man,

His struggle from the savage to the saint,

His yearning after justice, beauty, truth,

The simple steadfast power of welded wills,

The widening vision of the human soul

Once swathed in darkness—well may such foretell

A self-help stronger than the gripe of beast

Or bandit, surer than the wasteful strife

Of greed devouring greed.

      A mighty change,

Enfolded in the troubled womb of time,

Shapeth itself in silence; foolish hopes

And fond alarms disquiet faithless breasts;

Love waits the birth unfaltering.—The wise world

Hath not forgot how in a simple room

A Jewish craftsman with his fisher-friends

Once ate their farewell supper; high priests hissed

Their spite; Rome curled a lip of sickly scorn;

But life was with the little brother-band,

And mankind's slow salvation.—Love can wait.

DIES NON

The brooding halcyon hour is here at last;
    The world's tumultuous wrong has taken flight
    With that dark ocean-mood, which yesternight
        Did battle with the blast.

Heaven smiles to see its beauty in the bay;
    Care lies a-drowning where the blue tide laves
    The rust-red weed, and frolic of light waves
        Laughs heaviness away.

Fresh from the ripple's delicate caress,
    I lean upon the bosom of a rock,

That basks with me, forgetful of the shock
    Of storms, the sea's distress;

And listening, while the slow wave-crests unroll
    Their splendour, to the sea-mew's lonely cry,
    Sweet echoes of a sister melody
        Waken along my soul.

Once more I seem to hear the wood-dove croon
    In secret covert consecrate to spring,
    The whisper of the forest's half-fledged wing
        Fanning the flush of noon;

The long sea-murmur sweeping o'er a main
    Of billowy brake and glade, where sunshine dyes
    With touches of her tenderest harmonies
        The treetops' purple plain;

And once more through the oak-grove's hoary screen,
>   Beyond the faded fern, are caught afar
>   Glimpses of larchwood where the wind-flowers star
>   The thicket's early green.

Again I seek the time-worn stones that pent
>   A garden once, deep-sheltered from mankind,
>   Now haunted only by the homeless wind
>   And memory's low lament;

And musing watch the kestrel o'er his bower
>   Hover, with kingly pinions scarce astir,
>   The butterfly, spring's motley harbinger,
>   Sway on the sun-kissed flower;

Or mark the slender shadows rise and fall
>   Where in their silken cradles beech-leaves dream

Of summer's bridal, and the soft sunbeam

    Sleeps on the windless wall,

And warms to life the old romance that strays

    Forgotten where the rose-leaves mouldering lie,

And weds it with the gracious luxury

    That decks these fuller days—

The nestling grange that seems a friendlier part

    Of Nature's self, in outward guise akin

To some moss-suited crag, and clothed within

    By Nature's consort, Art;

There Welcome waits beside the ruddy glow

    That flecks the roof and laughs along the floor,

There Farewell passeth through the crowded door

    With lingering steps and slow;

There, ranged in carven shrines, rich caskets keep
　The embalmèd wisdom of the deathless dead,
　And music summons pity, love and dread
　　From out the spirit's deep;

Or while the wine-cup sparkles, thought's free tide
　Flows eddying onward, limpid, smooth, profound,
　Or leaping from the heights with sudden bound
　　Laugheth where shallows glide.

Care vexeth not, nor calumny molests
　The quiet of that home; but settled soft
　O'er roof and lawn, o'er bower and stream and
　　croft,
　A mellow gladness rests.

The squirrel on the daisy-freckled grass
　Sports unafraid; the poet's daffodil

Stoopeth to kiss his semblance in the rill;

And when spring's love-dreams pass,

Roses shall queen it, making every breath

A pant of joy; the peach shall sun her cheek

When bird-songs tire and hues of evening streak

The creeper's beauteous death.

Nor is the scene less fair when dead leaves lie

Thick in the pool's clear bosom, and the pines

Darken, and o'er the sodden meadow shines

A blue November sky;

Or when the bare boughs' livelier tints are lost

In black against the snow, and from the eaves

Hang ice-spears, and the holly's trim-cut leaves

Are edged and spiked with frost.

Ah! genial home! where every season lends
    Fresh grace, where hospitality's glad rites
    Bless, and the loving-cup of deep delights
        Circles among close friends.

There youth might twine the laurel and the rose,
    Manhood forget the world, and old age lull
    The soul to slumber, calm and beautiful
        As autumn's rich repose;

But that afar, where smothered with a pall
    Of vapour the great cities sweat and groan,
    From misery's dull heart a weary moan
        Ascendeth, marring all.

WELCOME TO THE QUEEN

On the occasion of Her Majesty's visit to Birmingham, in the year of Her Jubilee, to lay the foundation-stone of the Victoria Law Courts.

Hail! Mother of thy people! Hail!

Who deignest, in this golden year,

To lift awhile the widow's veil,

And with a sovereign smile to cheer

The gloom, that widening hour by hour

Enfolds the heart of England's toil,

The clouds that, ever gathering, lower

Above the clang of our turmoil.

Now wellnigh thirty years have lent
 A graver glory to thy brow,
Since last our barrier'd thousands rent
 The air with one vast welcome; now
The beard is grey of him who ran,
 Clasping his child, to gain a place;
And the child's self, a stalwart man,
 Shoulders his way to see thy face.

What though we miss the genial voice
 Of that pure soul, whose princely tone,
A nation's pride, love's simple choice,
 Made faultless music with thine own;
His gracious influence rules us yet,
 His memory still inspires our way,
And joy makes welcome of regret—
 His spirit lives with thine to-day.

Then brook, great Queen, thy people's glee;
    We cannot choose but let thee know
Our gladness in thy jubilee,
    The joy that makes our hearts o'erflow;
So once again this steadfast town
    Doffs for a day its sober dress,
Unknits the firmness of its frown,
    And revels wide in happiness.

So once again our paths are dense
    With myriads of thy strong ones; high
Throbs every pulse in rare suspense,
    And eager looks of loyalty
Crowd every casement; the gay streets,
    With flag-festoons and streamers hung,
Laugh out, and every steeple greets
    Its Sovereign with a rapturous tongue.

And now a happy murmur fills
    The air, till brass and drums give out
The nation's hymn;—each bosom thrills
    A moment;—then one mighty shout
Bursts from a thousand breasts, and drowns
    The ponderous chords, and ever moves
Beside thee as thou mov'st, and crowns
    Thee Victress of thy people's loves.

Despise not our rough welcome; we
    Know little here of cultured calm;
But in our reverence for thee
    To none will we forego the palm;
Ours is a hopeful discontent
    That slumbers not while harm is wrought,
A spirit stout and confident,
    And rugged ore of honest thought.

Here labour makes the daylight dark,
    And while night's roof of lurid smoke
Reflects the leaping furnace—hark!
    The giant hammer's thunder-stroke!—
Yet have we hearts as soft as strong,
    Hands ever swift to succour need,
Blood that can boil at tale of wrong,
    And heritage of manly deed.

Here dwelt the seer whose thoughtful eye
    First clove in twain Air's subtle stream;
Here mind's divine supremacy
    Tamed to our use the monster Steam;
And here Toil's nameless warriors give
    Their lives to yield the world increase,
And patient armaments achieve
    The bounteous victories of peace.

Then welcome, welcome! for thy reign
    Is rich with trophies, that shall last
When to a wiser world in vain
    Destruction sounds her frantic blast;
On lightning's wing our counsels flit,
    The ocean shrinks, the hills depart,
The power most swift to slay hath knit
    The nations into one great heart.

Now Knowledge sheds her quickening ray
    In darkest haunts, and selfless Skill
Hath woven many a spell to stay
    The progress of the powers of ill;
Truth lifts her head, Oppression quails,
    A purer air surrounds the throne;
And slowly o'er the land prevails
    The spirit of the Lord we own.

What though the shades of doubt affright,

    And God's new dayspring tarries long;

What though from dens of woe each night

    Ascends the cry of nameless wrong;

What though Want's ravening billow rolls

    Around the heedless isles of lust;

Never, to cope withal, were souls

    More earnest, tender, brave and just.

Then welcome! for thou com'st to found

    A Hall of Right. May Justice flow

Free through the realm, nor stagnate, bound

    In one choked well; that men may know

'Tis not for naught the sunlight dyes

    Our Hall with hues that speak thy fame,

While round us, far and wide, arise

    Memorials of thy glorious name!

Glorious in queenhood, for above
    The reach of malice shines thy power;
Glorious in womanhood, for love
    And noble sorrow are thy dower.—
Would that all English breasts, which swell
    Like ours with joy of jubilee,
Might mingle one full cheer, to tell
    The faith and love they bear to thee!

May no presaging dread molest
    The peace that broods around the shore
Of thy loved isle, though all the West
    Be dark with clouds of threatening war;
But may thy world-wide Empire, drawn
    To one close brotherhood, sustain
The promise of a holier dawn,
    The triumph of thy matchless reign!

SPRING SONG

The fragrance of awakening flowers
  Quickens the breath of Spring;
Exulting in their bridal bowers
  The mated wood-birds sing;
The lark is up; the gentle air
Carols light music everywhere.

The bee sings at her lovely toil,
  The cricket at his play;
The redbreast scans the fresh-turned soil;
  The meadows, pied with May,
Shimmer beneath the trembling blue.—
Since all is song, I warble too.

A CHRISTMAS CAROL

Cheerless, through dens of want and death,

Where unregarded woe blasphemes

The Lord in whom we boast our faith,

    The Christmas dayspring gleams.

Friend of the poor! that spak'st of one

Beside whose gate a lazar lay,

Dost mark the deeds of love undone

    Where Love is preached to-day?

The man that leaves thy poor in hell,

And saith to his fed heart, "Am I

My brother's keeper, so I dwell

    In halls that hear no cry?"

The noisome tree, whereof the fruit

Is pomp and lust, which fills the air

With pestilence, and hath its root

    In hunger and despair?

O Thou, whose smile the children knew!

Dost mark on yonder garret-bed,

Where weeps the rain the rafters through,

    Three starvelings, and one dead?

And him who lolls in Pleasure's lap,

With dice and wine and paramour,

And tosses in a jockey's cap

    The wages of the poor?

Avenging God! who woke at length,

A hundred years gone by, and gave

For one tremendous hour the strength

Of Samson to the slave;

And made repent in tears and blood

The harsh oppressors of the world—

How long, ere yet of Brotherhood

The banner be unfurled?

MORNING TWILIGHT

Sadly in the silent west,

The moon, worn-out with watching all the night

Over the sleeping earth, her cheek

Hollow and white,

Wan with a sorrow that she may not speak,

Sinks to her lonely rest.

Like a love-deserted maid,

That dare not meet her lord awake, but steals

By night to his bedside, to mourn

Her loss, and feels

Him waking, in the sunlight of his scorn

Triumphantly arrayed.

THE SEMPSTRESS TO HER SKYLARK

Poor little captive!—never more
    To seek the sunlight-hidden stars!—
I know what 'tis to break the heart,
    Searching the sky through prison-bars.

"O for a breath of ocean-air!
    O for a draught of morning dew
Fresh from the cowslip-cup, and bright
    With heaven's all-embracing blue!

"O for the speedwell's azure smile!
    O for the mountain's noonday sigh!

O for the clouds!"—and yet, dear lark,
　　Thou canst not love them more than I.

—Now cease to chafe that ruffled breast;
　　For by my sorrow, pretty sweet,
This very evening thou shalt rest
　　Beneath the moonbeams and the wheat.—

Farewell—farewell!—O for a friend
　　To do what I have done for thee!—
But patience!—though men's hearts are hard,
　　God's hand some day will set me free.

SEMPER EADEM

THREE hundred years have passed since Spain
 O'ershadowed thought's new dawn with fear,
And proudly forged a Titan's chain,
 And rattled it in Freedom's ear;
And dared upon the deep to flaunt
 The pomp of hate, the pride of creed,
And vexed our waves with idle vaunt—
 Lo now!—her sceptre is a reed.

They lie where storm and sea go forth
 To wage o'erhead eternal fight,
Where the foundations of the North
 Unshaken rest in voiceless night;

The rust hath eaten bolt and brand,

    With weed the wrecks are mantled o'er,

Those iron throats are choked with sand

    That roared against our native shore.

Yet not in Britain's golden days

    Were men united, save in deed;

For some deplored, with wistful gaze,

    The sunset of a parting creed,

And some desired the dawn; but all

    Uprose as one to face the foe,

And girt them at their country's call,

    And laid the bold invader low.

Three hundred years have passed, and Spain

    Wears yet the shackles of the priest,

And knout and famine goad in vain

    The sullen slave-hordes of the East;

The nations yet grow great in guilt,
    Aspiring but to overwhelm,
While restlessly, with hand on hilt,
    Suspicion scowls from realm to realm.

But who shall say old England grows
    Less hale, her sons of meaner mood?
Their life hath dyed the Russian snows,
    The desert sand hath drunk their blood;
Though valiant deeds no more are done
    With wings of white and oaken keel,
Each stands as steadfast to his gun,
    And iron ribs hold hearts of steel.

We fear no stranger. Our worst foe
    Teems in our midst, where in grim street,
Choked with Advancement's overflow,
    The eyes of Vice and Hunger meet;

Where myriads draw their joyless breath
> Only to sweat, and drink, and breed,
And haggard mothers drug to death
> The babes their bosom fails to feed.

Yet while hearts hotly swell, when Wrong
> Fastens upon his helpless prey,
And while eyes beam with light, that long
> To tear the mask of Fraud away;
While keen and watchful brains abide
> To cast the Future's horoscope,
And generous heirs of ease and pride
> Renounce their birthright—there is hope.

THE DEAD CAPTAIN

FALLEN !—we shall not see his sword again
Flash in the bitter conflict waged with wrong;
Nor hear his voice, amid the uncertain throng,
Call to his rallying comrades, not in vain.
The weakling lies not always with the slain,
The triumph is not always to the strong.
We question not the dark decree; we trust
'Twas well for him; for us 'tis well; the lust
For power and fame, the weakness to be great,
Are quelled with grief, and humbled to the dust,
Where by the simple bed Death holds his state.

WITH FLOWERS

If these smile bright, believe they know
   That beauty is a flower;
If crushed and drooping, they confess
   Thy smile's victorious power;
If they look pale, it is because
   They pined and paled for thee;
And if they blush, believe their hearts
   Are trembling consciously.
They wither, doomed through death alone
   To greet a flower more fair;
Yet, ere they perish, kiss them once,
   'Twill raise thine image there;

For often as thy fragrant breath

Is mingling with their scents,

There meet an angel and a flower,

Thine own pure elements.

A STORM SCENE

CRASH out, ye mighty chords!—The heavens are
    black
With wrath; the lightnings shudder through the air,
    And blind with fury tear
        The huddling rack,
Furling its pale and tattered banners o'er
        Yon steel expanse;
Tender as newborn love a rainbow glows,
The warm mist 'neath it flushes moist and rose
    City and sea and shore
        Steeped in one trance.

And every treetop sparkles with its leaves
    Refulgent in the setting sun;
The meads are golden-green, rich with the storm
    Of Nature's summer-love;
    Far in the night above
A white bird twinkles like a star, and cleaves
    The thunder-caverns dun;
Denser and louder forth the sullen tempests swarm.

Crash out, vast symphony!—thy lover hears
And worships.—It is over—those fierce tears
    Have blotted all to grey;
    With smothered moan
Great Nature's passion-music, like our own,
    Is sobbed away.

TO ONE IN SORROW

Patience! Time's gently-pressing palm
Is on thy wound. Thou canst not feel
The virtue of the looks that calm,
The quiet of the hands that heal;
 Yet some glad morning thou shalt rise
 To taste again Joy's sweet surprise.

So from the day that saw it fade
The plant takes heart. Thou canst not mark
The hueless bud, the wrinkled blade,
Forcing their prison cold and dark;
 Yet in some fostering, sunny hour
 Doth spring to life a newborn flower.

TO SWEET SEVENTEEN

To thee, young queen, these tribute lines
    Charged with my love—the word is writ ;
A daintier word were false ; but "love"
    No more can tell the soul of it,

Than "light" can tell the myriad mood
    Of sunshine ; from the fickle play
Which frolics through the dappled leaves
    When all the lanes are white with May,

To that full bliss of warmth which lies
    Delirious on the breast of June,

Or sunset flash of burdened heavens,

    Or dreamy glow of autumn noon.

So "love"—poor word—is all we have,

    To paint each radiant power that makes

The sunshine of a human heart;

    From the sweet sense of want which wakes

In childhood's breast, to ripe repose

    Of wedded faith, or ecstasy

Of passionate youth, or such delight

    As that I take, fair girl, in thee.

GRASS OF PARNASSUS

There is a flower, a milk-white star,
    That twinkles on the mountain-side,
Up-glancing where its sisters are,
    Sightless beyond the blue noontide.

One simple leaf, an emerald heart,
    Closes around its slender stem ;—
Not all the witchery of art
    Could fashion such a faultless gem.

Look on its snowy brow !—O see
    The tracery that veins its cheek !—

The faintly-flushed anemone

    Is not more delicate and meek.

Yet where the unbridled tempest blows—

    A sunbeam cradled in the storm—

It smiles in innocent repose,

    A peaceful, pure and perfect form.

AUTUMN SONG

The year grows heavy; but the hour
Is fresh as April; the blithe air
Is tremulous with sun and shower;
    A rainbow smiles farewell
To the spent storm, and everywhere
    Song breaks from hill and dell.

So when the summer of our life
Fades into autumn, now and then
An hour will come to us, sweet wife,
    When all our soul shall sing,
And all our heart shall leap, as when
    We drank the dew of Spring.

SERENADE

When moonlight o'er thy casement weaves

Its network through the breathless leaves,

And lake and lawn beneath the summer sky

Dream in the mist—

Ah! sweet! a lovelier scene within doth lie

By slumber kist.

And when the stars begin to pale,

And trampling on her crimson veil

Young Morning flashes forth with dewy hair

And sparkling eyes—

Ah! sweet! I linger for a dawn more fair,

When thou shalt rise.

www.ingramcontent.com/pod-product-compliance
Lightning Source LLC
Chambersburg PA
CBHW020249170426
43202CB00008B/288